GOURMET
HERBS

Classic and Unusual Herbs for
Your Garden and Your Table

Beth Hanson—Guest Editor

🍴

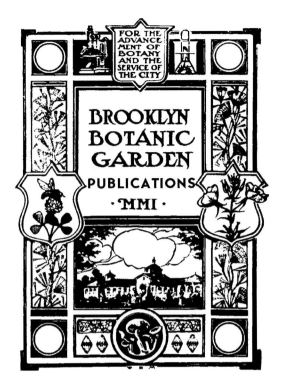

Janet Marinelli
SERIES EDITOR

Sigrun Wolff Saphire
ASSOCIATE EDITOR

Mark Tebbitt
SCIENCE EDITOR

Anne Garland
ART DIRECTOR

Steven Clemants
VICE-PRESIDENT, SCIENCE & PUBLICATIONS

Judith D. Zuk
PRESIDENT

Elizabeth Scholtz
DIRECTOR EMERITUS

Handbook #167
Copyright © Summer 2001 by the Brooklyn Botanic Garden, Inc.
Handbooks in the *21st-Century Gardening Series,* formerly *Plants & Gardens,*
are published quarterly at 1000 Washington Ave., Brooklyn, NY 11225.
Subscription included in Brooklyn Botanic Garden subscriber membership dues ($35.00 per year).
ISSN # 0362-5850   ISBN # 1-889538-21-3
Printed by Science Press, a division of the Mack Printing Group.
Printed on recycled paper.

TABLE OF
CONTENTS

INTRODUCTION

GROWING HERBS FOR EVERY OCCASION

BETH HANSON

🍴

CERTAIN PLANTS HAVE CHARACTERISTICS above and beyond the purely ornamental—a sharp or pleasing taste, a sweet or pungent aroma, the power to effect physiological change and perhaps to heal. After centuries of experimentation, people have incorporated these potent plants into their diets, rituals, and healing arts. These plants are the herbs. Because they have been so valued, herbs have traversed the globe in the pockets, pouches, boxes, and suitcases of their human admirers.

The herbs native to the stony, dry soils around the Mediterranean—rosemary, sage, thyme, bay, lavender—spread north and west with the soldiers and settlers of the Roman Empire, to gardens throughout Europe. Centuries later, the Europeans took those herbs with them when they set sail for the New World—and, in turn, sent back many new botanical discoveries to their homelands.

A new form of migration is under way: whole cuisines are on the move via restaurants, magazines, television, and the Internet. The North American cooking repertoire now includes dishes from places like India, Vietnam, Thailand, Japan, and Mexico—and international recipes are popping up in once-homogeneous venues such as the cookbook classic *Joy of Cooking*. And along with these new foods have appeared the herbs that make them unique.

One of the best ways to assure a ready supply of the often hard-to-obtain herbs at the heart of the new international cuisine—as well as a steady source of the better known herbs that are most tasty when they're fresh—is to grow them yourself, in your own herb garden. This volume focuses on culinary herbs that have a longstanding place in European and American cooking and those that are just becoming familiar. Take a tour

4

The best way to assure a supply of the unusual herbs at the heart of the new international cuisine is to grow them yourself. Familiar herbs like basil, above, are most tasty when they're fresh from the garden.

of the world and find out what people across the globe like to eat, and how they prepare it. When you finish reading the chapter on the uses of herbs and spices around the world, you will be better informed—and hungry.

Herb gardens provide not only a feast for the palate, but for the eyes as well. Whether you are planning an herb garden from scratch or tinkering with an established one, the chapter devoted to herb garden design will make you look at your garden in a new way. It touches on the history of herb gardens and the general principles of garden design, and it includes three basic designs, created especially for this book, that can be adapted to numerous garden situations.

Some of the more unusual herbs are available only from seed, and the chapter on seeds will help you get started. No need to worry if you have a restricted space for gardening—most herbs adapt beautifully to container growing. Learn how it's done in the chapter on container culture.

At the heart of this book is an encyclopedia of gourmet herbs, in which you will find written and pictorial portraits of dozens of herbs, as well as information on how to grow them and how to use them in various dishes.

You probably won't be able to use all of the herbs you harvest from your garden during the growing season, so it's useful to know how to keep them for the cool, winter months. Turn to the chapter on preserving herbs, and you will learn how to dry and freeze them, how to make herb vinegars and butters, and how to candy leaves and flowers, among other things.

Finally, herb suppliers' assortments have blossomed with gardeners' renewed interest in both culinary and medicinal herbs, and the list at the end of the book will point you to the best sources for herb seeds and plants.

HERBS AND SPICES AROUND THE WORLD

KARAN DAVIS CUTLER

🍴

GENERALIZING ABOUT ANYTHING IS DANGEROUS. (To generalize, the poet William Blake observed, "is to be an idiot.") But attempting to write about herbs and spices and how they're used in different cuisines in fewer than 700 pages requires generalizing, just as defining the difference between herbs and spices does. Because herbs and spices are intertwined in most cuisines, many dishes and traditions include both.

In general, we grow herbs for their green parts, that's to say for their leaves and stalks; we cultivate spices for their flowers, fruits, seeds, bark, and roots. *In general,* we use herbs fresh, and spices dried. *In general*, we agree on which is which: basil and parsley are herbs; saffron, the stigmas of *Crocus sativus*, and cinnamon, the bark of *Cinnamomum verum (C. zeylanicum)*, are spices. But there are plants that are both: used fresh, *Coriandrum sativum* is the herb cilantro, while the plant's dried seeds are the spice coriander. So take the generalizations that follow with a grain of salt—which, by the by, is a basic *taste* but neither an herb nor a spice. (Herbs and spices contain flavor, the combination of taste and aroma.)

A TASTE OF EUROPE

Many North Americans are most familiar with the herbs and spices popular in European kitchens. Thyme, tarragon, oregano, marjoram, parsley, sage, basil, bay, garlic, and rosemary are common in French and southern European cooking. A *bouquet garni*, which is nothing more than sprigs of thyme, bay, and parsley tied together, is *de rigueur* in countless French stews and other dishes. *Fines herbes*, equal amounts of fresh chopped chervil, chives, parsley, and tarragon, is used in soups, stews,

Dill dresses up fish and many other dishes popular in Northern and Eastern European kitchens, which also make ample use of parsley, caraway, and thyme, among others.

meat dishes, and more, and so is *herbes de Provence*, a mix of equal parts dried basil, fennel seed, lavender, marjoram, rosemary, sage, summer savory, and thyme.

In Italy, oregano, basil, and garlic are a near-holy trinity, commonly used in both fresh and cooked dishes. Spain and Portugal use fewer herbs than most of their Mediterranean neighbors, but no one should take a trip to Spain without sampling *paella*, the traditional rice and seafood dish that is seasoned with saffron. Or leave Portugal or Madeira without having tasted *espetada*, beef kebabs flavored with bay, or laurel.

In Northern and Eastern Europe, dill, mint, parsley, caraway, thyme, horseradish, sorrel, fennel, and paprika are everyday ingredients—as well as garlic, that ubiquitous kitchen herb. Dilled horseradish-mustard sauce is popular in many regional cuisines in this area of the world, served with cold meats, fish, hard-boiled eggs, and sliced cucumbers and tomatoes. Garlic is the predominant flavor in *tarator*, a cold Bulgarian soup made from cucumbers, ground walnuts, and yogurt, while the Russian cucumber soup *rassolnik* is made with fennel. Beet soup, or *borscht*, is traditionally flavored with dill, parsley, and lovage; Romania's traditional clear-broth soup, known as *chorbe*, depends on lovage for its tang but may also contain dill, parsley, coriander, chives, and garlic. New potatoes dressed with dill are a popular dish in Finland. Dill is everyday

fare in many Scandinavian dishes—in fact, the word dill comes from the Old Norse *dilla*, which means "to lull to sleep."

NORTH AFRICAN AND MIDDLE EASTERN FLAVORING

Europe has lost some of its glamour as the culinary Mecca these days. With the shrinking of the globe through international travel and advances in communication, food lovers have developed a zest for the cuisines of other parts of the world, such as North Africa, Southeast Asia, and the South Pacific. So, empty your bottles of *herbes de Provence* and refill them with *dukka*, an Egyptian spice blend of sesame seeds, roasted chickpeas, coriander, cumin, and mint, or with *garam masala*, a blend from northern India that includes cinnamon, bay, cumin, coriander, cardamom, peppercorns, cloves, and mace.

Middle Eastern kitchens use a wide variety of flavorings, perhaps a reflection of the many cultures that call the region home. The emphasis is on spices, aniseed, allspice, caraway, cardamom, cassia, coriander, clove, cumin, dill, fennel, fenugreek, ginger root, nutmeg, saffron, sumac, and more. Basil, cilantro, garlic, marjoram, mint, parsley, rosemary, sage, and

Opposite: Sage, a native of the Mediterranean, is a staple in European cuisines.
Right: Curry, *Murraya koenigii,* is a must in the spice blends of South Indian cooking.

HERB AND SPICE MEDLEYS

BOUQUET GARNI: sprigs of thyme, bay, and parsley tied together
CHERMOULA: puréed cilantro, parsley, garlic, cumin, paprika, saffron, lemon juice, and olive oil
CURRY POWDER: chiles, coriander, cumin, curry leaf, mustard seed, peppercorns, fenugreek, ginger, and turmeric
DUKKA: sesame seeds, roasted chickpeas, coriander, cumin, and mint
FINES HERBES: fresh chopped chervil, chives, parsley, and tarragon
GARAM MASALA: cinnamon, bay, cumin, coriander, cardamom, peppercorns, cloves, and mace
HERBES DE PROVENCE: equal parts dried basil, fennel seed, lavender, marjoram, rosemary, sage, summer savory, and thyme
LA KAMA: ginger, cumin, nutmeg, turmeric, and black pepper

thyme are commonly used fresh herbs. *Hilbeh,* a Yemeni sauce, derives its flavor from fenugreek and coriander; *harissa,* a tongue-searing sauce from Tunisia, contains garlic, caraway, cumin, coriander, and mint as well as chile peppers. *Falafel,* the popular Middle Eastern street food made of puréed chickpeas, is seasoned with garlic, parsley, coriander, and cumin, shaped into small patties, and fried in hot oil.

Garlic is probably the most common flavoring in Greek and Turkish foods, essential to the olive-based sauces *skorthalia* (Greece) and *tarator* (Turkey). Garlic and mint are used to flavor the familiar cucumber-yogurt dish, which is called *tzatziki* in Greece, and *çaçik* in Turkey. In the more moderate climate of

SOUTHERN EUROPE: BRUSCHETTA

This popular Italian appetizer from Tuscany is so good that you may want to double the recipe and forget about a main course. The bread can be toasted in the oven, or you can toast it outdoors over a gas or charcoal grill. To taste its best, bruschetta must be made with high-quality bread and olive oil, and with vine-ripened tomatoes.

FOR THE FLAVORED OIL:
⅓ cup olive oil
3 Tbsp. finely chopped fresh basil
2 cloves garlic, finely chopped
2 tsp. finely chopped oregano

FOR THE TOPPING:
6–8 fresh plum tomatoes, or 2–3 large tomatoes
2 Tbsp. finely chopped fresh basil
1 Tbsp. olive oil
1 clove garlic, minced
salt and pepper to taste

12 slices Italian bread

TO MAKE THE FLAVORED OIL: In a glass bowl, combine oil, basil, garlic, and oregano; cover and let stand at room temperature for at least 2 hours.
TO MAKE THE TOPPING: Chop tomatoes and place in a glass bowl. Add basil, oil, garlic, and salt and pepper and let stand at room temperature about 1 hour. Pour off liquid before using.
TO PREPARE THE BRUSCHETTA: Brush bread with flavored oil. Toast bread on both sides until golden. Serve hot with topping.
Serves 4–6.

Clockwise from top left: Chervil, chives, parsley, and tarragon. Used together they are known as *fines herbes* in French cooking, where they flavor soups, stews, meat dishes, and more.

NORTH AFRICA: CHICKPEA & LENTIL SOUP

Peas and beans are the mainstay of hearty soups in North Africa, including this one. The secret of this simple recipe lies in the herbs and spices and in the quality of the chicken stock. If the word chickpea is unfamiliar, you probably know this legume as garbanzo bean, its other common name.

2 Tbsp. olive oil
1 large onion, coarsely chopped
3 cloves garlic, finely chopped
6 cups chicken stock
1 cup dried lentils
1 cup canned chickpeas, not drained
1 tsp. cumin
2–3 Tbsp. finely chopped fresh mint
2 Tbsp. chopped fresh parsley
1 Tbsp. fresh lemon juice
zest of ½ lemon, finely chopped
1 cup fresh cilantro, coarsely chopped
salt and pepper to taste
lemon wedges for garnish

In a heavy saucepan, sauté the onion and garlic in the oil over medium heat until the onion turns golden. Add lentils and stock, lemon zest, and a generous pinch of freshly ground pepper and simmer, uncovered, over low heat until lentils are tender, about 40 minutes. Add chickpeas, cumin, mint, and parsley, and cook for 10 minutes longer. Remove from heat, and stir in lemon juice and cilantro. Add salt to taste, garnish with lemon wedges, and serve.
Serves 6.

Greece, dill, marjoram, oregano, and mint are widely grown and used; in Turkey, spices tend to predominate, especially allspice, cumin, and cinnamon.

In North Africa, saffron, cumin, paprika, turmeric, ginger, cardamom, cassia, mace, chiles, nutmeg, and garlic are standard fare. Moroccan cooks purée cilantro, parsley, garlic, cumin, paprika, and saffron with lemon juice and olive oil to make *chermoula*, a sauce well-matched with grilled chicken or fish; *la kama*, a mixture of ginger, cumin, nutmeg, turmeric, and black pepper, is used to flavor stews and soups. *Couscous*, the North African dish that is now a common offering at deli counters, is typically made with coriander, cumin, ginger, cinnamon, and turmeric.

Couscous looks like a grain but it's actually a type of pasta. Pasta and grain dishes are very common throughout the world. Rice is used in India to make *pilau* or *pilaf*, which is flavored with a five-spice mixture (cumin, black cumin, mustard, fennel, and fenugreek) called *panch phora. Jollof*, a pilaf-like dish from West Africa, can be made with cloves, cumin, garlic, ginger, mint, paprika, thyme, or other herbs and spices. In Indonesia, *nasi kuning*, a yellow-rice dish prepared to mark happy occasions, uses lemon grass, turmeric, and salam leaves.

In Iran, even simple rice dishes such as *chelow* are prepared with saffron, while in Mexico you may encounter green rice, *arroz verde*, made with chiles, parsley, epazote, and garlic.

SOUTHEAST ASIAN FLAVORINGS

Garlic is an essential ingredient in many Thai recipes, as are chile peppers (*prik nam som*, or chiles in rice vinegar, is a well-known condiment); tamarind, zedoary, lemon grass, ginger, basil, cilantro, and mint are also common ingredients. Thai chefs often mix a half-dozen herbs and spices with coconut milk to produce complex flavors in curry dishes. Vietnamese cuisine is distinguished by the very large amounts of herbs used, especially dill,

Top: Ginger, cultivated for its roots and thus considered a spice, not an herb, is important all over Asia. Bottom: The stalks of lemon grass add a refreshing zing to many Southeast Asian dishes.

lemon grass, cilantro, mint, and basil. *Pho bo*, a beef-and-noodle soup that is eaten any time of day, is served with lime wedges and generous bowls of fresh herbs, including chiles, cilantro, mint, and basil. *Com hung giang*, a spicy Vietnamese rice dish containing shrimp, is flavored with lemon grass, garlic, chile peppers, scallions, onions, Vietnamese fish sauce, and shallots, and garnished with cilantro.

Even an abridged list of spices and herbs used everyday in Indonesian cooking is impressive: Cinnamon, cloves, coriander, cumin, curry leaf (*Murraya koenigii*), chiles, garlic, ginger, lemon grass, nutmeg, and turmeric are the names most of us know. Less familiar—or completely unfamiliar—are kenchur root, laos root, and tamarind. A typical dish is a vegetable soup made with coconut milk and flavored with garlic, ginger, chiles, lemon grass, and turmeric. Tamarind, which has a sour, fruity flavor, is also used in the Philippines, as are garlic, chiles, star anise, cloves, cinnamon, ginger, turmeric, nutmeg, rosemary, and dill.

A TASTE OF INDIA, CHINA, AND JAPAN

Indians use almost as many herbs and spices as languages (15 major and more than 1,000 minor languages). Tradition has it that to be a good cook in India, one must first be a good *masalchi*, or blender of spices. Basic curry blends, most characteristic of southern Indian cooking, are likely to

HERBAL BROTH

You can use an herbal broth instead of chicken or beef stock in almost any recipe. The result will be just as delicious.

Simply simmer vegetables and herbs in water until they are soft and their flavors and nutrients have been released. While you're chopping vegetables, decide which herbs you're in the mood for. The options are endless: a *bouquet garni*, *fines herbes*, or *herbes de Provence* simmered with the vegetables impart a lovely flavor. Some herbs, like basil, cilantro, parsley, and dill are very good sprinkled on the finished broth. For a more assertive taste, add some garlic cloves. For Asian flavors, try ginger or lemon grass.

To make 2 quarts vegetable stock add the following ingredients to 10 cups of water in a large pot, bring to a boil, and simmer, covered for 45 minutes. Strain.

2 large unpeeled potatoes, cubed; 2 large carrots or parsnips, peeled and sliced; 1 large onion, quartered; 1 celery stalk or celeriac, chopped; 1 apple or pear, seeded and chopped; 1 bay leaf; 10 peppercorns; and herbs of your choice.

—*Sigrun Wolff Saphire*

SOUTHEAST ASIA: **SATÉ**

A saté, or satay, is a popular Southeast Asian dish of skewered, grilled meat that is traditionally served with a peanut dipping sauce. The marinade in this recipe—every region in the area has its own version—comes from Indonesia and can be used with chicken, beef, lamb, or pork. The word saté comes from the Javanese verb meaning "to stick."

4 shallots, chopped
3 Tbsp. light soy sauce
2 Tbsp. vegetable oil
1 Tbsp. fresh lemon juice
1 Tbsp. brown sugar
4 cloves garlic, crushed
1 tsp. coriander
½ tsp. salt
1 pound meat (chicken, beef, lamb, or pork) cut in cubes

In a glass bowl, combine the oil, shallots, soy sauce, lemon juice, sugar, garlic, coriander, and salt, and mix well. Pour over the meat cubes and cover; let marinate in the refrigerator for at least 4 hours. Thread the meat cubes on bamboo skewers that have been soaked in water and grill over high heat until meat is thoroughly cooked. Serve with peanut sauce. Serves 2–4.

PEANUT SAUCE

2 tsp. minced fresh ginger
2 serrano or jalapeño chiles, seeded and finely chopped
1 clove garlic, finely chopped
3 scallions, finely chopped (including tops)
⅓ cup chunky peanut butter
⅓ cup coconut milk
3 Tbsp. light soy sauce
1 Tbsp. lime juice
3 tsp. brown sugar

Combine the ginger, chiles, garlic, scallions, peanut butter, coconut milk, soy sauce, lime juice, and sugar in a small pan. Bring to a boil over medium heat, stirring frequently, then reduce heat and simmer, uncovered, until slightly thickened, about 10 minutes. Remove from heat. Add more coconut milk if the sauce is too thick to pour. Adjust seasonings to taste and serve at room temperature.

include chiles, coriander, cumin, curry leaf, mustard, peppercorns, fenu-greek, ginger, and turmeric. *Garam masala*, one of the primary spice blends used in the north, contains cinnamon, bay, cumin, coriander, car-damom, peppercorns, cloves, and mace. In eastern India, cooks blend cumin, fennel, mustard, nigella, and fenugreek to form a mixture called *panch phora*. Which flavorings are used most often throughout India? Probably garlic, mint, cilantro, and ginger.

Two of the world's most popular cuisines—those of China and Japan—are nearly herb-free zones. In Chinese cooking, ginger, chiles, cloves, star anise, and garlic are used sparingly; herbs are even rarer in Japanese kitchens, where the emphasis is on unadorned flavors. Korean cooks add

HERB BLENDS: PRINCIPLES AND PROCEDURES

Culinary herbs can be divided into two main flavor groups—mild and robust. The annual herbs are typically mild while perennials tend to be robust. Basil, chervil, dill, and parsley are some of the more delicate-tasting annuals. Robust perennials, which generally have woody stems, include rosemary, sage, savory, tarragon, and thyme. This division is not perfect: some annuals like coriander and summer savory have strong flavors, while some perennials, such as marjoram and bay, are mild. Mild and robust do not always refer to the taste of the fresh leaves; mild also describes herbs that combine well in cooking, or whose flavors soften in cooking.

Robust herbs are hardy and their flavors remain strong even when cooked for a long time. Use them together or singly for braised or

Culinary herbs are divided into two flavor groups—mild and robust. The perennial rosemary at left is considered a robust herb: it retains its strong flavor even when cooked for a long time. The flavors of mild herbs are more delicate and soften in cooking. Most mild herbs are annuals, such as basil, chervil, and dill.

herbs with a heavier hand, especially garlic, ginger, and chiles, which are combined with fermented soybeans to make *kochujang*, a popular flavoring.

THE FLAVORS OF SOUTH AND CENTRAL AMERICA AND THE CARIBBEAN

In the Caribbean and South America, the chile is king, with cilantro, parsley, annatto, allspice, and garlic playing secondary roles. In Mexico, annatto, avocado leaves, bay, cinnamon, cilantro and coriander, epazote, garlic, hoja santa, onions, and Mexican oregano (Spanish thyme) are used often, but none as often as chiles. Serranos are the favored pepper for *gua-*

roasted meats or poultry, and in soups or stews, or combine them with basil, marjoram, or other mild herbs.

You can use milder herbs in larger amounts and with more variation. Combine two or three in one dish if their flavors are complementary. These mild-mannered herbs are good in salads and dishes in which the leaves are raw or cooked for only a short time. A little too much of a fresh herb probably won't ruin a dish, but too many herbs in one dish may clash, or the flavors may become muddied.

Experiment with the herbs that appeal to you most and that you think might work well together. When combining herbs, learn to trust your sense of taste. A blend of two or three herbs usually provides enough interest and balance for most dishes. But complex dishes like long-simmering soups or stews may use up to four or five herbs, in the form of a *bouquet garni,* for example.

When you dry an herb, some, but not all, of its oils are concentrated. This means some flavor elements will be stronger, while the fragrance may be weaker. The nuances and balance are not the same as in fresh herbs. Use about one-third the amount of a mild dried herb as you would use fresh. For example, use a teaspoon of dried marjoram or a tablespoon of fresh, minced leaves. Use the dried leaves of robust herbs carefully. You may need only half a teaspoon of dried sage, rosemary, or thyme in place of a tablespoon of the fresh minced herb.

For maximum flavor, crumble the dried leaves as you add them to a dish to release their essential oils. If the dried herbs are fairly fresh, their taste will be strong. Add a small amount, simmer, taste, and adjust as needed. Usually a teaspoon is enough to flavor an entire dish.

—*Susan Belsinger*

camole and *salsa de tomate verde cruda,* which is made with green tomatoes. Jalapeños are used for stuffing and smoked to become *chiles chipotles.* Poblanos are typically charred and peeled before they're stuffed with meat or cheese for *chiles rellenos* or added to salads and soups. When ripe and dried, the poblano is called a *chile ancho*; it is the most common chile in Mexican kitchens. Güeros are used for pickling and to flavor stews; and habaneros are used to produce sauces hot enough to make a gringo cry for mercy.

A final generalization: few things have traveled the globe more widely than herbs and spices. Basil, cilantro, dill, garlic, parsley, and mint, to mention only a half dozen, are common culinary commodities everywhere. No surprise, perhaps, for the spice trade began at least 5,000 years ago. So it's only a matter of time until American garden centers offer tamarind trees and we're all tucking epazote and zedoary between the rosemary and the thyme in our gardens. 🍴

THE AMERICAS: ARROZ VERDE

Arroz verde, or green rice, is a visual treat from the Puebla region of Mexico. This recipe comes from Karen Hursh Graber, a native New Yorker who maintains a web site crammed with recipes and information about Mexican cuisine (www.mexconnect.com), as well as a great guide to the herbs and spices used south of the border.

1 cup raw rice
2 Tbsp. vegetable oil
3 small or 2 large poblano chiles, roasted, seeded, and peeled
½ medium onion, chopped
2–3 sprigs fresh parsley
2–3 sprigs fresh epazote
2–3 cloves garlic
2½ cups chicken or vegetable broth
½ cup fresh or thawed frozen peas (optional)

Soak the rice in hot water for 15 minutes, then rinse in a strainer under running water. Drain rice and let dry.

Purée the chiles, onion, garlic, parsley, epazote with ½ cup of the broth in a blender or food processor.

Heat the oil in a large skillet. Add rice and sauté it, stirring frequently, until golden. Add the purée, mixing well; add the remaining 2 cups of broth. Cover and simmer over low heat until all the liquid has been absorbed. Remove from heat and add peas. Salt to taste.

Serves 6.

COLORS, SCENTS,
CONTOURS, AND CONTRASTS

DESIGNING
AN HERB GARDEN

GWEN BARCLAY AND MADALENE HILL

MENTION HERBS and many people think of medieval monastery gardens. In most of these gardens monks planted neat, individual beds of small vegetables and fruits, always making sure to include medicinal herbs, so important to them in their healing arts. The early monastic herb garden design probably

Following a formal European design tradition favoring symmetry and straight lines, this herb garden is arranged around a central focal point.

19

Left: The rounded shapes of *Santolina* and variegated sages lend themselves to the elaborate design of a knot garden, in which plants are arranged to give the illusion that they are woven into knot patterns. Opposite: Just as beautiful, but much less work-intensive, is an informal garden design incorporating contrasts in colors, heights, and textures.

served as the basis for the classic *potager* of Europe, and especially France, a utilitarian garden of vegetables and kitchen herbs. Its name is derived from *potage*, the French word for thick soup, a primary food in the Middle Ages. The monks' approach is well suited to a collection of herbs today, provided you have enough space for individual beds devoted to a solid planting of a single herb.

But it is the traditional four-square design, favored for cloistered gardens at large churches, that has become the standard for modern herb gardens. Sometimes called the four-quarter or quadripartite motif, its origin is shrouded in the dim mists of antiquity. This simple ancient design has long been imbued with the rich religious and literary symbolism of the number four. The four beds originally represented the four rivers of paradise as described in the bible and later came to symbolize the four elements—fire, water, air, and earth. The Botanical Garden at the University of Padua, Italy (1543) uses the motif in a circular form. Following European explorations in the 16th and 17th centuries, the four beds came to represent the four continents known at the time—Asia, Africa, the Americas, and Europe.

The basic quadripartite geometric configuration, interpreted as squares, rectangles, circles, or triangles, with the center often marked by a pool or water fountain, has remained popular throughout garden history because it is pleasing to the eye, easy to maintain, and readily adapted to garden spaces of any size.

But gardeners in the new millennium needn't be bound by tradition. In many gardens today, culinary herbs and colorful, edible flowers are arranged artistically in the vegetable garden among the carrots, beans, and tomatoes. The popular cottage garden design enables people with small lots to create a lush, informal landscape that's perfect for the soft colors and textures of herbs—with the heavenly fragrance thrown in as a bonus. You can also tuck herbs in among the shrubs and flowering plants in border beds or grow them alongside a walkway or even the garage wall.

PLAN AHEAD

It is always wise to begin garden planning with an accurate drawing of the site, especially if you envision much actual construction. Drawing a picture of all the available space may help you arrive at unexpected design solutions. Take into account the architecture of the house, existing trees and shrubs, and the topography of the site. Consider the available sunlight and air circulation. Ideally, you want to incorporate a structure that can help frame or enclose the garden, such as a garage, summerhouse, greenhouse, or barn. Divide large spaces into smaller sections and add pathways to provide access for maintenance and harvesting. Finally, be sure the garden is located where you can enjoy it as much as possible in each season of the year.

FORMAL DESIGNS

Formal gardens favor symmetry and straight lines: they usually have a clearly determined central axis or a focal point around which forms and elements are arranged. They achieve symmetrical balance with mirror-like plantings on either side of the axis or around the center, which might contain a small tree, fountain, sculpture, or sundial. The beds usually have borders made up of tightly clipped plants like boxwood, thyme, or other sub-shrubs. Within the beds, plants are often set in rows or geometric patterns, or dozens of the same plant are installed together creating a carpet effect. Perimeters and walkways are usually laid with brick or other paving materials, making a formal garden a rather expensive proposition.

The classic four-square mentioned above is one of the most common formal herb garden designs. Even more elaborate is the knot garden, a

By tucking culinary herbs and edible flowers in among the chards, carrots, and squashes, gardeners with small plots can create a lush and fragrant landscape.

formal design in which plants are arranged to give the illusion that they are woven into knot patterns. Herbs that have naturally rounded shapes or are easily pruned, such as santolina, lavender, thyme, and germander, lend themselves to this design. They are also useful as borders in small beds, as in the classic *parterre* associated with palace pleasure gardens, a geometric arrangement of gardens separated by a pattern of walks or grass.

Knot gardens are beautiful and traditional, but they are high-maintenance endeavors and should not be undertaken lightly, as the plants require constant pruning. This is a particular problem in the South, where long, hot summers trigger many plants to take a nap. If woody, shrub-like herbs are hard-pruned when they are dormant in hot weather, they will not sprout new growth and may die. If you garden in the South, choose plants—preferably evergreens—that tolerate light pruning in hot weather. These include boxwood, holly, and other small-leafed, woody landscape plants. Alternately, consider using annuals

continues on page 28

HERB GARDEN DESIGN:
FOUR-SQUARE

The basic four-square, the most common formal herb garden design, is easy to maintain and readily adapted to garden spaces of any size. In the design shown above, the squares (each measuring nine feet by nine feet) are planted with herbs from four culinary regions: Western Europe, Asia, southwestern U.S. and Mexico, and Mediterranean. The number of plants you need for each bed depends on the size that you make your garden. Use seasonal annuals to fill in around slower growing perennials. If you live in an area of extreme winter cold or summer heat, consult a local authority, such as your Cooperative Extension office, about varieties suitable for your climate. In warm regions, alternate cool-weather loving herbs with those that like long hot, summers.

PLANTS FOR THE FOUR-SQUARE HERB GARDEN

WESTERN EUROPEAN GARDEN
(upper left)
 1 Sweet basil
 2 Dill
 3 Onion chives
 4 Coriander
 5 Greek oregano
 6 Curly parsley
 7 Rosemary
 8 Sweet marjoram
 9 French thyme or
    English thyme
10 Lemon thyme
11 Silver thyme
12 Gold thyme
13 Sage
14 Golden sage
15 Tricolor sage
16 Purple sage
18 Nasturtium
19 Mint (in container)—
    spearmint or peppermint
20 Arugula or roquette
21 Lemon balm
22 Lavender

ASIAN GARDEN
(lower left)
 1 French thyme
 2 Houttuynia
 3/3a Cinnamon basil or
    licorice basil
 4 Thai basil
 5 Lemon grass
    (in container)
 6 Ginger
 7 Turmeric
    (*Curcuma longa*)
 8 Galangal
    (*Alpinia galanga*)
 9 La lot (*Piper
    sarmentosum*)
10 Vietnamese coriander
11 Culantro or ngo gai
12 Asian celery

13 Cuban oregano
14 Perilla or tia to
15 Rau ngo or rau om
16 Garlic chives
17 Leeks
18 Coriander
19 Red-stem apple mint
20 Vietnamese balm
21 Chile pepper
22 Edible chrysanthemum
23 Leech lime
    (*Citrus hystrix*)
24 Onion chives

SOUTHWESTERN/ MEXICAN GARDEN
(upper right)
 1 Sweet bay
 2 Italian flat-leafed parsley
 3 French thyme
 4 Mexican basil
 5 Spicy globe basil
 6 Coriander
 7 Culantro or ngo gai
 8 Garlic
 9 Onion chives
10 Lemon verbena
11 Garlic chives
12 Chile pepper
13 Papalo (*Porophyllum
    ruderale*)
14 Fennel
15 Mexican mint marigold
16 Dill
17 Rosemary
18 Arugula or roquette
19 Epazote
20 Lemon balm
21 Sweet marjoram
22 Spearmint (in container)
23 Oregano
24 Sage
25 Burnet
26 French sorrel
27 Borage
28 Calendula

29 Daylily
30 Rose geranium
31 Mexican mint marigold
32 Nasturtium
33 Rose

MEDITERRANEAN GARDEN
(lower right)
 1 Sweet bay
 2 Lemon balm
 3 Basil
 4 Borage
 5 Chervil
 6 Chives
 7 Coriander
 8 Dill
 9 Fennel
10 Parsley
11 Lovage
12 Horseradish, variegated
13 Sweet marjoram
14 Spearmint
15 Oregano
16 Arugula or roquette
17 Rosemary
18 Winter savory
19 Burnet
20 French tarragon
21 Mexican mint marigold
22 French thyme
23 Sage

CENTER DIAMOND
The diamond measures four feet by four feet and has a brick or stone border
    Rosemary
    Caraway thyme or
       creeping thyme of choice

Note: Botanical names are provided only for some plants not discussed in the book. Please refer to the index for the scientific names of all other herbs.

HERB GARDEN DESIGN:
INFORMAL

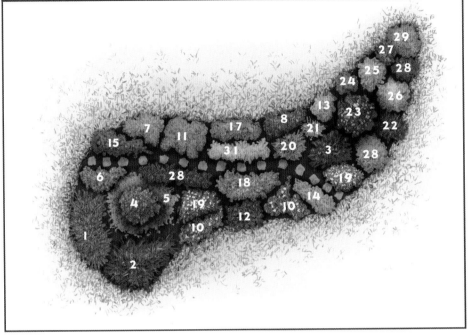

An informal bed makes a beautiful herb garden. Featuring a rose bush as an off-center focus, this full-sun garden works best if it is raised at least eight inches above the ground. When starting from scratch, use a garden hose to outline a pleasing shape. (The plan above is for a garden roughly 16 feet wide.)

PLANTS FOR THE INFORMAL HERB GARDEN

1 Lavender
2 Prostrate rosemary
3 Upright rosemary
4 Bay
5 Creeping golden oregano
6 Tricolor sage
7 Dwarf garden sage
8 Purple garden sage
9 Mexican mint marigold or French tarragon
10 Nasturtium

11 Greek oregano
12 Italian oregano
13 Green lemon thyme
14 Golden lemon thyme
15 French thyme
16 Caraway thyme
17 Curly parsley
18 Italian parsley
19 Winter savory
20 Onion chives
21 Dill

22 Coriander
23 Fragrant antique rose for pillar, such as 'Zephirine Drouhin Pink', 'Climbing American Beauty Pink', 'Cramoisi Superieur Red'
24 Lemon balm
25 Cinnamon basil
26 Sweet basil
27 Lemon basil

HERB GARDEN DESIGN:
THEME CONTAINERS

Assemble your favorite herbs into containers to create a space-saving, easily accessible garden. In the design shown above, three whiskey barrel halves were each planted according to a theme, with herbs for salads, soups, and pizza, respectively. You may also want to try planting individual containers with mint, lemon grass, lemon balm, bay, chile peppers, and ginger.

PLANTS FOR THE THEME CONTAINER GARDEN

HERBS FOR SALADS
1 Parsley
2 Burnet
3 Chervil
4 Nasturtium
5 Mesclun (salad greens)
6 Dill
7 Basil
8 Onion chives

HERBS FOR SOUPS
1 Lovage
2 Dwarf sage
3 Curly parsley
4 Greek oregano
5 English thyme
6 Bay

HERBS FOR PIZZA
1 Oregano
2 Piccolo basil
3 Curly parsley
4 Prostrate rosemary
5 Sage
6 Fennel
7 Garlic chives

such as basil or biennial parsley for borders or knot designs, and replace them at the end of their life cycle.

Knot gardens can include a focal point such as a sundial or sculpture, or the knot itself can be the centerpiece of a larger herb garden. The focal point of a formal herb garden should be located at the center of the design. Try using a small herbal "tree" or standard such as sassafras, vitex, or witch hazel, or a large shrub rose, surrounded by lower-growing herbs of varying flower and foliage color. You can fill in the pattern with other plants, ideally of one variety, or you can cover the ground with gravel in different colors for contrast.

A focal point, such as this sundial in a bed of fragrant lavender, provides a striking accent in an informal planting.

INFORMAL PLANTINGS

Most gardeners do not have the time, inclination, or pocketbook needed to maintain formal gardens with or without a knot design. An informal arrangement, one that includes broad curving borders, free-form beds, or narrow beds lining walkways or outbuildings, is often a more realistic approach. Informal plantings are also an excellent way to link a wooded area to the remainder of your garden, or to take advantage of space around trees, which can shelter shade-tolerant herbs under their boughs. To help decide on the design of your informal planting, use a long garden

THEME GARDENS

One interesting way to design an herb garden is to organize it around a theme. Following are four ideas.

DOORWAY GARDEN
Devote a small doorway garden or an arrangement of containers to herbs, and they will provide you with an ample and easily accessible harvest for many tasty meals. Make room for English, French, or lemon thyme, summer or winter savory, French tarragon, or its fine Southern alternative, Mexican mint marigold, along with chives, parsley, mint, oregano, and basil, of course.

SALAD GARDEN
Culinary herbs planted with cabbage, chives, kale, lettuces, Italian parsley, salad burnet, tarragon, and edible nasturtiums and *Dianthus* make creating salads an exercise in good taste.

PIZZA GARDEN
Pizza's favorite seasonings of basil, oregano, rosemary, and thyme planted with tomatoes in a wheel-shaped garden will delight the entire family and perhaps get children interested in tending herbs.

FRAGRANT GARDEN
Fragrant plants are becoming more popular as gardeners learn that fragrance can come not only from flowers but from foliage, seeds and fruit, bark, and roots as well. A lovely antique rose such as *Rosa* 'Old Blush' might be the focal point of such a garden. Basil, dianthus, lavenders, rosemary, scented geraniums, and violets combine nicely for a delightfully fragrant planting that also serves to attract bees and butterflies.

hose to outline various potential shapes.

If the informal planting is backed by a fence or wall and therefore faces towards one side, group the herbs according to height: low or creeping (under one foot), mid-size (one to three feet), and tall (over three feet). Plant the tallest towards the back and the shortest towards the front of the beds. Assemble plants in odd-numbered clumps of three, five, or seven specimens rather than in straight lines. Use taller herbs, especially those with a beautiful or architectural form, as accents, to break up groupings of lower-growing herbs and to lift the eye. Tall ornamentals can fulfill the same function. In long borders, repeat plants that have strong flower or foliage color to unify the garden. If you like a riot of color, be sure to use enough of each strong color to make a statement.

THE DIRT ON SOIL

Regardless of where you garden, be sure to provide your herbs with well-drained soil. Most herbs do not like wet feet and will quickly die in standing water after a heavy rain. This is critical in the hot, humid climates of the southeastern and south central states, where deluges are common in summer.

Among herbs, only mints thrive in wet soil. Lavender and rosemary, both natives of Mediterranean climates, do best in soils that are dry and drain quickly after rain or watering. Parsleys, dills, and fennels will be at their most vigorous when grown in loose soils that have been amended with compost or other organic matter.

If your soil is heavy and drainage is a problem, consider installing raised beds. Built at least eight inches above ground level and filled with good topsoil, raised beds quickly solve most drainage problems.

You can grow most herbs successfully whether your soil is somewhat acidic or alkaline. Almost all herbs are most tasty and fragrant when they are grown in a soil or planting medium that is not overly rich, so avoid heavy applications of chemical fertilizers. Light applications of balanced organic fertilizers (with an N-P-K formula of 10-10-10, for example) or compost early in the spring and again in late summer are all that herbs require—and they probably will thrive without any fertilizer at all.

Mulch the soil after planting to conserve water and suppress weeds: use whatever organic mulch is readily available in your area. Smaller-sized pieces are usually more attractive with herbs, so avoid the so-called "nuggets." Organic mulches will need to be replenished occasionally because they literally compost into the soil. Experiment with gravel or crushed granite mulch for Mediterranean-type herbs, which prefer a drier environment.

Tie the planting together with low bordering herbs; in no time their soft growth will spill over the edges, enhancing the feeling of curving shapes. Informal plantings are especially effective for large raised beds, wall gardens, or sloping ground.

In free-standing beds, focal points should be located off-center to encourage viewing from different vantage points. Consider incorporating some type of water feature in the garden. The sound of water is soothing and restful, and as a bonus, water attracts wildlife.

Like many gardeners, you may opt for a combination of formal and informal designs. You can have the feel of a formal garden by dividing the space into smaller areas outlined by simple borders, while at the same time arranging the herbs informally within the beds.

COMBINING HERBS

If you are planning a new garden area, make a wish list of plants you would like to grow, noting each plant's sun and moisture requirements and growth habit—including height and width at maturity. First-time gardeners often do not allow enough room for perennial plants to develop to their full potential. Some herbs eventually tower at several feet, while others remain low and creep along the ground. For the first few years you can fill in any gaps with annual herbs and flowers while the perennial herbs put down good foundation roots and get ready for expansion.

As in any garden, plants in an herb garden should be arranged in aesthetically pleasing combinations. Contrast rounded and soft plants with stiff and spiky growth—and take full advantage of the many shades of gray and green foliage. Bear in mind, though, that some herbs require more frequent watering than others: moisture-lovers, such as all varieties of basil, mints, lemon balm, monardas, nepetas, parsley, and tansy, should not be grouped with drought-tolerant sages, thymes, lavender, rosemary, and oregano, which all like drier feet. Also, beware of exuberant herbs, which can take over a garden, crowding out less aggressive varieties. It's a good idea, for example, to grow all species of mint in large containers, and never more than one variety to a pot! Herbs such as *Artemisia ludoviciana* 'Silver King' and many monardas also deserve a wide berth in the garden and ruthless control.

GROWING HERBS IN CONTAINERS

BARBARA PERRY LAWTON

GIVEN A ROOMY POT and a location with four to six or more hours of sun each day, most garden herbs will thrive in containers. If you live in an apartment and your growing space is limited to a small balcony or windowsill, or if your garden is not very spacious, try growing herbs in containers. You can also use potted herbs to decorate a patio or pool area, softening the texture of bricks or paving stones with beautiful greenery.

Herbs with compact growth patterns are the most attractive candidates for containers. Dwarf sage and the basil cultivar 'Spicy Globe' are both ideal for containers in- or out-of-doors. You can grow larger-leafed basils in pots too, but keep a tight rein on them by clipping their growing tips every few days; these snippets are perfect for tomato sandwiches, *pesto*, and salads.

Because most varieties tend to be compact, thymes of all sorts—including creeping thymes, which trail prettily over the edges of pots—are good prospects for containers, as are chives (*Allium schoenoprasum*) and Chinese or garlic chives (*A. tuberosum*), whose attractive, linear growth

Opposite: Their compact growth makes chives ideal container plants.
Right: Plant lemon grass in a pot and move it indoors in winter for year-round harvest.

Flue tiles buried in the garden keep the roots of aggressive herbs in check, preventing rambling wanderers like mint from taking over the garden.

stops at 18 inches. Don't forget marjoram, an elegant, tender herb with oregano-like scent and flavor, and winter and summer savories, both tidy plants appropriate for planters.

Tender herbs are obvious choices for pots and containers, since they don't survive the winter in cold climates. The tender culinary sages, gold *(Salvia officinalis* 'Icterina'), purple ('Purpurascens'), and tricolor ('Tricolor'), offer unusual foliage colors as well as tasty delights for the culinary palette. Also among my favorites for container growing are lavender, rosemary, sweet bay, and Greek myrtle. They are handsome and respond well to pruning, and most forms are tender north of Zone 7. I like to grow these plants outdoors in the summer and take them inside during the cold seasons. For a more formal look, you can shape them into herbal topiaries with judicious pruning and pinching.

Dwarf dills such as 'Fernleaf' provide a feathery, see-through look that can be very effective in a pot. French tarragon, a must for serious cooks, adapts well to planters, too. The true mints, rambling wanderers, can be a plague if set free in the garden, so grow them in pots. Spearmint, peppermint, apple mint, and pineapple mint are all rewarding pot plants. If they become lanky, prune them back severely. Once they are growing in a tidy fashion, be sure to nip their tips regularly. Eat the aromatic foliage, or use it in arrangements or as a fresh potpourri to bring the heavenly fragrance into your home.

THE INDOOR HERB GARDEN

Although most herbs are at their very best in sunny garden sites, many will grow quite well in containers inside. Sufficient light is key to indoor growing. Herbs will get leggy and weak if they get too little light.

There are many ways to increase indoor light and keep your herbs healthy. Standard fluorescent tubes and track lighting are widely available, and more recently, round fluorescent bulbs that screw into lamps like incandescent bulbs have come on the market. Check your nursery or hardware store for the latest developments in lighting. If you don't want to bother with artificial lighting, you often can extend the fresh-herb season by at least two to three months by simply bringing the plants indoors and putting them by a bright window. Summer savory, the tender lavenders, rosemary, sweet bay, and Greek myrtle all make good indoor companions. Mints do well indoors because they don't require as much light as many other herbs. Unless you have a large sunny atrium or a greenhouse with lots of room and plenty of light, avoid large herbs like lovage and angelica.

Beware of overwatering. Never water by the calendar. Instead, let the condition of the soil guide you. Allow the soil to dry to the touch, then water until it runs out of the holes in the bottom of the container; never let herbs sit in a saucer of water! You can purchase an inexpensive moisture meter to help you monitor the soil in large containers. Herbs need little fertilizer indoors or out.

Although the strong scents of herbs usually repel pests, including aphids, mealy bugs, and spider mites, examine the plants carefully for pests and diseases when you bring them indoors or home from the nursery. Once inside, isolate the herbs for seven to ten days before putting them near other indoor plants. This practice will cut down on winter plant problems.

MIX AND MATCH

When planting in containers, you have many design choices. Group, regroup, and rearrange herbs planted singly in containers, or plant several herbs in larger containers, which make important statements on doorsteps, balconies, and patios, or along garden paths.

Some gardeners like to group herbs in pots according to their uses—see "Theme Gardens," page 29. Others like to mix containers of herbs with containers of flowering annuals. I gather my ready-to-plant containers and fresh-from-the-nursery herbs, then experiment with plants, containers, and combinations. Some plant combinations are especially attractive: creeping thyme makes a great groundcover under rosemary, Greek myrtle, or bay trees

When planting in containers you have many design choices. Try experimenting with plants and containers until you come up with the combinations you like best.

trained as topiary standards. The colors and textures of dwarf sage and marjoram mix well. Summer savory and chives together make a bold design statement. The tender variegated sages combine well in large containers with the gray-green, hardy culinary sages. The feathery dwarf dills create a pleasing contrast to compact, mounding herbs such as 'Spicy Globe' basil.

A GARDEN CONTAINED

In the hot South, a slick trick is to grow the popular summer sweet basil by itself in a large container. In late summer, drop some dill or coriander seeds in the container. The basil will keep the seeds moist until they germinate when the weather cools. As the basil season winds down and the plant finishes its life cycle, the cool-weather lovers dill and coriander will be ready to use. In early spring, reverse the process and drop basil seeds into the container or plant purchased seedlings. In warmer parts of the country the dill and coriander will survive the winter and help protect the tender basil from late-season cold snaps.

—*Gwen Barclay and Madalene Hill*

PLEASING POTS

Clay pots, glazed pots, plastic pots, wash tubs, half barrels, drainage pipes, flue tiles, and an endless assortment of rather oddball choices—consider all of these categories when choosing a container. Think about the style of your home, inside and out: if it tends toward traditional, you may want to try large, terra cotta or plastic foam containers

A container planted with a collection of your favorite herbs and placed next to your doorstep guarantees easy pickings in inclement weather.

that come in classic Tuscan or traditional English designs, in shades of red or gray. If your home and garden are more modern in style, consider the clean lines of flue tiles, whether rectangular or round. Patio arrangements made up of glazed and unglazed flue tiles in several sizes and heights can be handsome and unusual. Larger tiles are heavy and will be hard to move once planted, so it's best to plan ahead and place them where you want them. Since both rectangular and round flue tiles are bottomless, decide where to put them before filling them with the planting medium. Smaller ones can be plugged at the base with hardware cloth or screening and moved around on a rolling stand. Also consider baked clay drainage and sewer tiles, which come in various diameters and colors. Many building supply companies carry them and will cut them to the desired lengths.

A variety of manufactured planters are now available, including window boxes in many sizes and styles, sturdy plastic containers that straddle balcony and deck railings, and self-watering planters with water reservoirs—a good choice for those who are away often. Then there are the oddball planters—such things as children's wagons, wheelbarrows, and down-home tractor tires turned inside out with pinked edges. I've even seen buckets, old boots, nail kegs, and an automobile hood used as planters.

Make sure that planters with solid bottoms have enough holes for good drainage, which is essential for most herbs. Remember that larger containers won't dry out as fast as smaller ones on hot, windy days, and that clay pots allow air and moisture to pass through and therefore dry out faster than impervious containers.

STARTING HERBS FROM SEED

HOLLY SHIMIZU

GROWING HERBS FROM SEED is a great way to produce plants in abundance. It's easy, and more economical than buying herb plants from a nursery or garden center. What's more, some herbs such as dill, coriander, and chervil are best propagated this way because these short-lived annuals resent transplanting. Be sure to buy seeds from a source with an excellent reputation (see "Seed and Plant Sources," page 104), so that you know your seeds will be viable and come from parent plants with great flavor and vigor.

The best way to grow most herbs from seed is to start them in a con-

trolled indoor environment in early spring and then transplant the seedlings into pots, giving them the chance to become vigorous before moving them to the garden outside. This is particularly true for slow germinators like parsley, which takes several weeks to germinate. Parsley seeds contain chemicals that inhibit their germination. This feature prevents the seeds from all germinating at the same time or when

Left: As soon as the first true leaves appear, gently move seedlings from flats to individual pots. Opposite: For easy identification, use labels when you plant seeds.

environmental conditions are not quite right.

If your seeds do not germinate well, it may be for a variety of reasons. Seed companies harvest the seeds of most herbs when the largest percentage of seeds is ripe, but on most herb plants, seeds do not ripen all at the same time. Check your seed packages for a germination rate; this will help you decide how many seeds to sow to get the desired number of plants. The life span of herb seeds is variable. Among others, parsley, chive, and coriander seeds are rather short-lived. Check the dates on the seed packages before you buy them, and label seed collected from your own garden with date and name.

Some herbs should not be propagated from seed. French tarragon, for example, rarely produces flowers and is virtually sterile. Among thymes, lavenders, rosemaries, mints, and many cultivars of oregano, there is so much genetic variability that you cannot count on good flavor and fragrance when you grow them from seed, so it is always best to propagate these herbs from cuttings or divisions.

A HEAD START

When to start herb seeds depends on the hardiness of the herb and its speed of growth. You can start herbs that prefer cool weather, such as

Depending on the size and the shape of the seeds, a sieve or a screen can be a helpful tool when separating mature seeds from chaff.

angelica and lovage, outside before the last frost date without damage, but hold tender (cold-sensitive) herbs such as basil and nasturtium back until the weather (and therefore the soil) has warmed up some.

When planting seeds indoors, use new containers or sterilize used ones by washing them with a mixture of one part bleach to nine parts water. (Propagation trays with clear domes are a good choice; they are available in most hardware stores and can be reused year after year.) Since garden soil tends to be heavy and may carry viruses and harmful bacteria, start your seeds in a soilless mix, such as Pro Mix BX or Cornell Mix B. These sterile mixes are made from natural materials including vermiculite, perlite, composted bark, composted peanut hulls, and sphagnum peat moss. Moisten the mix before sowing the seeds so that it is damp but not soggy.

Do not cover tiny seeds such as those of thyme and basil with soil; just spread the seeds on top of the mix and scratch in. Cover larger seeds such as nasturtium or coriander with soil twice their thickness when you plant them in pots, flats, or cells. You will need to *scarify* some herb seeds—that is to say, you need to soften or break their hard, thick seed coats by soaking the seeds in water or scratching their coats with a file. (For example, I soak nasturtium seed in hot water for 24 hours before sowing.) Scarifying allows water and gases to diffuse into the seed, helping the plant embryo to break through the coating.

SAVING SEEDS

Seeds become *viable*—able to grow into new plants—when they are mature. Seeds are mature and ready to be collected when they turn brown, which will likely be in summer and fall. Cut the stems that have a seed head and invert them into a paper bag. Place the bags in a dry area for at least a week, until the seeds are completely dry. Then separate the seeds from the chaff. Depending on size and shape of the seeds, a sieve can be a helpful tool in this process. Store the seeds in airtight containers in a dry, cool area. Keep in mind that excess humidity or high temperatures can destroy seeds within a few days. I like to save my seeds in old film containers, always making sure to label them with the exact name of the plant and the date of harvest.

Most herbs are wind- and insect-pollinated, and when the pollen is transferred from the anther of one flower to the stigma of a flower on another plant (cross-pollination), the resulting seeds may grow into plants that are different from the parent. You can prevent cross-pollination by covering the flowers with paper bags to block pollination, or plant closely related herbs that might cross-pollinate far apart.

Make sure that container and soil drain adequately, because soggy soil will deprive your seedlings of the oxygen they need for the proper growth and development of their root systems. Once the seedlings have germinated, monitor the soil carefully for moisture. If the seed flats dry out, the young seedlings will die. Water with a gentle spray when you notice that the soilless mix becomes lighter in color, indicating dryness.

As your seedlings grow, observe them closely. If you notice that some of the seedlings are falling over, they may be suffering from damping-off, a fungal disease that attacks seedling stems, constricting water and nutrient transport to the leaves. It often occurs in patches, and can happen very rapidly. However, there are some steps you can take to help prevent damping-off: ventilate your seedlings by increasing the flow of air that surrounds them, make sure they are not overly crowded, water in the morning, and be sure that the soil is well aerated.

LET THERE BE LIGHT

Most herb seeds do not need light to germinate, but they all need light as soon as they emerge. The ideal sunlight for seedlings is moderate exposure. Room light is usually sufficient. If the light intensity is not strong enough, your seedlings will become spindly. Move them to a brighter win-

Once your transplanted herb seedlings fill their pots, it's time to harden them off. Put them in a cold frame that you keep open during the day and close at night.

dow or to a spot under grow lights. During late winter when the intensity and length of natural light are not sufficient for emerging herbs, grow lights make all the difference, giving you a jump on the gardening season. The main equipment you will need is a set of fluorescent lights. Use one warm-white tube and one cool-white tube in a fixture placed approximately eight inches above the flats; keep them on for 12 to 16 hours a day. As soon as the first true leaves appear, transplant the seedlings to 2- or 2½-inch pots, taking care not to hurt the seedlings' delicate root systems; do this promptly or your seedlings may get leggy and tangled.

Once your plants fill in the pot they are ready to be hardened off. This is the process that prepares the young, tender plants for the harsher outdoor environment. If you have a cold frame, use it for this purpose, keeping it open during the day so plants will acclimate and toughen up and closing it at night—especially if there will be a frost—to protect them from extreme cold. Otherwise, you can harden plants off by placing them outside in a spot where they will receive morning sun, then bring them back inside at night. If you do this for one week, your plants should be tough enough for planting outside. Some gardeners harden their young seedlings by placing them under spun-bonded row covers to protect them from the elements; this material keeps the sun and wind at bay and prevents frost damage but allows rain to come through.

Mulch the soil after setting the seedlings out in the garden to conserve water and suppress weeds. You can use whatever organic mulch is readily available in your area.

IN THE GREAT OUTDOORS

Starting seeds outdoors, in their permanent spot in the herb garden, has real advantages for herbs that resent transplanting, and is an efficient way to let annuals reseed (see the chart on this page). Once the seeds of annuals mature (they will become brown and hard), spread the seeds over the ground, then cultivate so that they are covered with some soil. Either later in the summer or in the following spring, new herb plants will appear.

STARTING HERBS FROM SEED

Common name Botanical name	Annual, biennial, or perennial	Start indoors or outdoors?	Reseeds readily?
Angelica Angelica archangelica	biennial (refrigerate seed to keep fresh)	indoors	yes
Anise Pimpinella anisum	annual	indoors	no
Anise hyssop Agastache foeniculum	short-lived perennial	outdoors	yes
Arugula Eruca vesicaria ssp. sativa	annual	outdoors	yes
Basil Ocimum basilicum	annual or tender perennial	indoors	no
Black mustard Brassica nigra	annual	indoors or outdoors	yes
Borage Borago officinalis	annual	indoors	no
Burnet Sanguisorba minor	short-lived perennial	indoors	no
Caraway Carum carvi	annual or biennial	outdoors	yes
Catnip Nepeta cataria	perennial	indoors	rarely
Chervil Anthriscus cerefolium	annual	outdoors	yes
Chicory Cichorium intybus	short-lived perennial	indoors or outdoors	yes
Coriander (Cilantro) Coriandrum sativum	annual	outdoors	yes

When planting herb seeds from packets directly in the garden, place them three to four times their thickness down into the soil. Follow the guidelines on the seed packet to determine the planting date; if you start them too early, when the soil is too cold or wet, the seed can rot. As seedlings emerge, thin them out so that they will be appropriately spaced and have room to grow. Check the seed packet for the proper spacing of each herb. As you thin, always leave the strong, vigorous seedlings and thin out the weaker plants.

Common name Botanical name	Annual, biennial, or perennial	Start indoors or outdoors?	Reseeds readily?
Culantro *Eryngium foetidum*	tender perennial	indoors	no
Dill *Anethum graveolens*	annual	outdoors	yes
Epazote *Chenopodium ambrosioides*	annual	indoors or outdoors	yes
Fennel *Foeniculum vulgare*	short-lived perennial	outdoors	yes
Fenugreek *Trigonella foenum-graecum*	annual	indoors	no
Nasturtium *Tropaeolum majus*	annual	indoors or outdoors	yes
Nigella *Nigella sativa*	annual	outdoors	yes
Parsley *Petroselinum crispum*	biennial	indoors	no
Perilla *Perilla frutescens*	annual	indoors or outdoors	yes
Purslane *Portulaca oleracea*	annual	indoors or outdoors	yes
Sorrel *Rumex acetosa*	perennial	indoors	no
Summer savory *Satureja hortensis*	annual	outdoors	no
Winter savory *Satureja montana*	perennial	indoors	no

THE TASTE OF SUMMER YEAR-ROUND

SUSAN BELSINGER

IN SUMMER, HERBS ARE ABUNDANT and achieve their peak flavor. Like most growing things, they are best when fresh and in season, but you can preserve your summer bounty of herbs in your freezer and pantry, capturing their flavor for the winter months.

About once a month during the summer, cut herbs back to encourage new growth and maximize your leaf harvest. You can cut perennials back to about one-third their height and most annuals to just above the bottom set of two leaves. The more you cut back your plants, the more leaves they will produce. At your final harvest of annual herbs, pull up the entire plants, tidying the garden for winter at the same time that you gather your bounty. Time your last harvest of perennial herbs about six to eight weeks before you expect a hard freeze in your area, giving the plants time to put out some

Opposite and right: Preserve summer's bounty of herbs for the winter months: herbal vinegars and dried herbs are just two options.

Left: Cut herbs back about once a month during the summer to encourage new growth and maximize leaf harvest. Opposite: Choose a sunny day for harvesting and pick the herbs in the morning after the dew has dried but before the hot sun evaporates their volatile essential oils.

new growth. Don't prune your perennial herbs later than that, as it will weaken their resistance to cold.

Herbs have the best flavor if they're harvested just before they bloom. Once plants start to flower, they send more of their oils to the blossoms and less to the leaves, which results in less flavor. Choose a sunny day for harvesting and pick the herbs in the morning after the dew has dried but before the hot sun evaporates their volatile essential oils. Do not leave the cut herbs out in the sun; take them to a shady area to sort and tie into bunches. If you pull up entire plants, cut off the roots. Remove the brown bottom leaves and any spotted or bug-eaten ones. If the herbs are dirty, brush away the dirt. If you must wash them, rinse quickly and pat them dry. You might want to spread them out in front of a fan to remove excess moisture quickly.

HANG THEM OUT TO DRY

You can dry herbs by hanging them in bunches or by spreading them on screens or in shallow baskets. If you decide to hang the herbs up, tie the stalks into small bundles with string or twine. Hang them in a dry, well-ventilated place out of the sun. A shed or an attic is usually a good place. If you are

drying herbs on screens or in baskets, remove large leaves from their stems before spreading them out. Keep the leaves of plants with small leaves, like thyme or savory, or needle-like ones like rosemary, on their stems.

If you are drying herbs for their seeds—to eat or save for next year's planting—be sure that the seeds are ripe. On many plants, including coriander, fennel, and dill, the seeds will turn from green to tan or light brown when ripe. Hang the herbs to dry as described above. Since the plants will drop some of their seed as they dry, hang the bunches over a screen or inside a paper bag with a few air holes cut in it.

The herbs will take from a few days to two weeks to dry, depending on the climate and humidity. Check them every day: if you leave them too long, especially in humid weather, they will turn brown. You can tell when the plants are dry by rubbing a leaf between your fingers; a completely dried herb will crackle and crumble. If it bends and is not crisp, it still contains some moisture. To remove the last bit of moisture, preheat the oven to its lowest temperature, not higher than 200° F., then turn it off. Spread the herbs on baking sheets and place them in the warm oven for about five minutes. Repeat if necessary.

When the herbs are fully dried, strip whole leaves from their stems and pack them in clean jars with tight-fitting lids. (If the herbs are not completely dried when you pack them in jars they will mold and spoil.) For the fullest flavor, pack the leaves whole; do not crumble them, as this will release their essential oils. Label the jars and store them away from heat

If you are drying herbs on screens or in baskets, remove large leaves from their stems before spreading them out. Keep the leaves of plants with small leaves, like thyme, or needle-like ones like rosemary, on their stems.

and light. You can store your home-dried herbs for about a year—until next summer's crop will take their place.

THE DEEP FREEZE

The flavor of most herbs does not survive freezing well enough to make the process worth the effort. Leaves often become dark and mushy as freezing temperatures break down their cell structures. Tender-leaved herbs form ice crystals that make them watery after a month or two in the freezer. Sturdy-leaved herbs such as sage and rosemary taste better when dried. Some herbs are best preserved in vinegar, but more about that later.

If you want to extend the season by a short time, or have an abundance of herbs you just can't bear to waste, use the following procedures for the best freezer results. Harvest and clean the herbs as instructed for drying. It's simplest to freeze whole leaves, which will also yield the best flavor. Remove leaves from the stems and pack them in small, airtight freezer containers or pint freezer bags. Label the containers, as herbs tend to look alike once frozen. You can also pack the herbs in larger containers; first freeze the whole leaves individually on

If you are drying herbs for their seeds—to eat or save for next year's planting—be sure that the seeds are ripe. On many plants, including coriander, shown above, the seeds will turn from green to tan or light brown when ripe.

baking sheets, then transfer them to the containers. Use leaves as you need them.

Many herbs freeze well when chopped and mixed with a little oil. If you know how you will be using the herbs, you can freeze mixtures of herbs—chopped basil and parsley together with olive oil for *salsa verde* or *pesto,* for example. If you plan to use the herbs in cooked dishes, try adding small amounts of stronger flavored herbs like marjoram, savory, or thyme to a blend. The flavors of these herbs hold up well to cooking. Or chop excess mints or lemon balm and cover with vegetable or canola oil and add the herbs to baked goods such as cookies or pound cake during the winter months. Herbs frozen in oil are best stored in tightly closed, half-cup to cup-size containers.

Keep herbs preserved in oil in the freezer, not the refrigerator. Botulism, a form of acute food poisoning caused by soilborne bacteria, can find its way into the kitchen on herb leaves and other plants. It isn't a problem when you use the herbs fresh, because it takes any *Botulinum* spores that may be present about two weeks to produce their toxin—which they can and will do even in refrigerated oil. (They will not grow in vinegar, which is highly acidic.) Your freezer is cold enough to store herbs in oil safely.

Herbs will take from a few days to two weeks to dry, depending on the climate and the humidity.

HERB VINEGARS

Herbal vinegar infusions are a simple way to concentrate herb flavor and preserve it for the winter—and they are a pleasure to make. All you need do for this agreeable satisfaction is harvest sprigs of your favorite herbs when they are at their aromatic peak and put them into vinegar for about four weeks. Bottles of brightly-colored opal basil vinegar and tarragon vinegar are two summer traditions that are considered kitchen wealth. They will enhance salads and sauces throughout the year. Experiment with different herbs when making vinegars: often a combination of two or three herbs offers a pleasant surprise.

PRESERVED TARRAGON

The French preserve whole tarragon sprigs for later use by pickling them in vinegar. Fill pint-size canning jars with washed sprigs of tarragon and cover with white wine vinegar. Seal the jars and store in a pantry or cupboard away from light and let stand for three to four weeks before using. Refrigerate the jars as you open them, and use the same amount of the pickled herb as you would the fresh. You can use the vinegar as well. For a stronger flavored tarragon vinegar, bring the desired quantity of good-quality white wine vinegar just to the boil. Decant it into bottles that are half-filled with fresh healthy tarragon sprigs. Cap and store at least three weeks before using. You can also use the sprigs from this concoction as you would the pickled tarragon.

Some excellent herbal choices for making vinegars are: anise hyssop, basil (especially the purple varieties), chive with blossoms, dill, lavender, all of the lemon herbs, lovage, mint, oregano, tarragon, and savory. A few favorite combos are chile peppers with oregano, sage, or thyme; a blend of some of the lemon herbs including lemon balm, lemon grass, lemon thyme, and/or lemon verbena with fresh gingerroot; and chive and dill with nasturtium flowers. A rule of thumb: never combine more than two or three herbs in a vinegar because the flavors tend to become muddy.

Good quality white wine or rice vinegars make the best herb vinegars. Apple cider vinegar also works well with the

To make herb vinegar pick sprigs of your favorite herbs and put them into vinegar for four weeks.

flavors of many herbs, but will not give the clean, bright colors that you get with a clear vinegar. Red wine vinegar is too strong for most herbs, and distilled vinegar is too harsh. However, some people prefer robust herbs such as oregano, rosemary, or even chiles with red wine vinegar. Experiment if this appeals to you. If you use distilled vinegar, buy a good brand, and dilute it by about one-quarter with distilled water to make it less harsh.

Harvest your herbs on a sunny morning, clean the sprigs if necessary, and pat them dry. Fill clean jars about one-half to three-quarters full with the herbs you have chosen and cover them with vinegar. Before you screw the lid on, cover the mouth of the jar with plastic wrap. Set the jars out in the sun and let it do its work to infuse the herbs and vinegar for three to four weeks. Then, bring the jars inside and strain the vinegar to remove the herbs. Pour the vinegar into smaller bottles, adding a fresh sprig of the herb if desired, and label. Store the vinegars in a cool, dark place and use them within a year.

HERBAL INFUSIONS

An infusion is an extraction of herb leaves or seeds used as a tea or to flavor drinks, alcohol, and vinegars. Herbs (both leaves and flowers) that work
well in infusions include mint, lemon balm or lemon verbena, and monarda.
You can drink infusions hot, like tea, or chill them and serve as you would
iced tea. You can also mix them with other drinks such as fruit juices, or
pour them into ice cube trays and freeze; use these ice cubes to flavor all
sorts of beverages. Use lemon basil or lemon balm ice cubes in lemonade

Mint, lemon balm or lemon verbena, and bergamot are some of the herbs that work
well in infusions, which taste delicious hot or chilled.

CANDIED HERBS

The following recipe will coat quite a few leaves and flowers; if you need more, mix up a second batch. (If you are worried about salmonella, use pasteurized, powdered egg whites, which are available in the baking section of the grocery store.)

Wax paper
1 extra-large egg white, at room temperature
Few drops of water
About 1 cup superfine sugar
Rinsed and dried herb leaves and flowers
A few small paint brushes

Spread a sheet of wax paper on a baking rack. In a small bowl combine the egg white with the water and beat lightly with a fork or small whisk until the white just shows a few bubbles. Put the sugar in a shallow dish.

Holding a leaf or flower in one hand, dip a paint brush into the egg white and gently paint it. Cover the leaf or flower completely, but not excessively. Hold the leaf or flower over the sugar dish and gently sprinkle sugar evenly all over on both sides. Place the leaf or flower on the wax paper

Candied flowers and herb leaves have been used for centuries to garnish fancy desserts, tea cakes, and more.

to dry. Continue with the rest of the herbs.

Let the leaves and flowers dry for 12 to 36 hours, depending on humidity; they should be completely free of moisture. Turn them once or twice during drying to make sure they dry evenly on both sides. To hasten drying, place overnight in an oven with a pilot light, or for a few hours in a very low oven (about 150 to 200° F.), with the door ajar. Store the dried, candied leaves and flowers between layers of wax paper in airtight containers until ready to use. They can be kept for up to one year.

HERBED ICE CUBES

Generous 2 cups packed fresh herb leaves; flowers can also be used
1 quart water

Bring the water to a boil in a non-reactive saucepan. Add the herb leaves and cover. Let steep for about 30 minutes, or until the infusion cools down to room temperature. Strain the herbs and pour the infusion into a glass jar or pitcher and refrigerate, or pour the infusion into ice cube trays and freeze until hard. Once frozen, pop the cubes into freezer bags, and label.

Makes about one quart of infusion; fills 2 or 3 ice cube trays.

or iced tea, mint ice cubes in iced tea or fruit juice, and basil ice cubes in tomato or vegetable juice or even *gazpacho*. Just be sure to label your freezer bags of ice cubes, because once frozen, the cubes all look the same.

HERB BUTTERS

Flavored butters are a staple of cooking and are delicious with a number of foods, from bread, pancakes, waffles, and pasta to every type of vegetable and fish. They are simple to make, and keep in the refrigerator for about a week or in the freezer for up to three months. Basil, chive, coriander, dill, fennel, lemon balm, marjoram, nasturtium leaves and flowers, tarragon, and thyme all make flavorful butters. Try experimenting with your favorite herbs; you may want to add an edible flower for color. A single herb, or a blend of two herbs, is generally best for flavoring an herb butter.

To prepare ½ cup of herb butter, soften 1 stick of unsalted butter. Finely chop or cut the herbs into a chiffonade, which is made by cutting herb leaves crosswise into thin strips to make narrow, ribbon-like pieces; about 2 tablespoons of herbs to ½ cup butter is a good ratio. Blend the herbs with the butter. You may want to add a bit of salt or pepper, lemon juice, or even minced garlic or shallots, depending on how you will use the butter. Pack into a small crock and refrigerate or freeze until ready to use.

CANDIED HERB LEAVES AND FLOWERS

Candied flowers and herb leaves have been used for centuries to garnish fancy desserts, *petits fours*, tea cakes, wedding cakes, and more. Candied herb leaves are often served after a meal, offered alone as a confection. The best leaves for candying are anise hyssop, the mints, lemon balm and lemon verbena, and pineapple sage. Good herb flowers for candying are borage flowers, scented geraniums, rose petals, and the violas. The job is easy but it takes a little patience; it is more fun if you do it with a friend (see the recipe on page 55).

ENCYCLOPEDIA OF GOURMET HERBS

SUSAN BELSINGER
AND KATHLEEN FISHER

ON THE FOLLOWING PAGES you will find detailed portraits of dozens of herbs, many of them probably familiar, and some you may not have encountered before, at least not in the context of cooking. Browse through this section to learn what the various herbs look like, what they need to grow best, and how to use them in the kitchen. Note the hardiness zones for perennial herbs to help you decide which plants are likely candidates to survive winter conditions in your area and which herbs you might want to move indoors during the colder months. A map of the USDA hardiness zones appears on page 103.

ANISE
Pimpinella anisum

Annual

Young anise plants have round, toothed leaves similar to those of flat-leaf parsley, but the new leaves of mature plants are almost fernlike. In the middle of the summer anise produces umbels of tiny, off-white flowers typical of other members of the carrot family, and later the little licorice-flavored, grayish brown seeds that give the Greek liqueur ouzo its "oomph" and are used to flavor licorice candy.

HOW TO GROW Cold-climate gardeners can start anise indoors in peat pots, and southerners can try sowing the seeds in fall. In Zones 5 to 7, sow anise seeds directly in the garden in spring once the soil and air are warm, ¼ to ½ inch deep, thinning seedlings to about 8 inches apart. Since these plants have weak stems, you might want to try even closer spacing to keep them more upright. Anise grows best in full sun, and light, fast-draining, deeply worked soil. It often rebels in hot, humid climates, and it doesn't like wind or competition from weeds, either.

CULINARY USES The parts used most often in cooking are the seeds. Have them on hand in winter to steam with root vegetables, such as turnips, parsnips, and carrots; add them to dishes featuring cabbage and its relatives;

Agastache foeniculum, **anise hyssop.**

stew them with fruits; or use them to flavor muffins and cookies. During the growing season, the fresh leaves lend flavor to salads, sauces, and soups. Anise is a famous breath freshener, so keep it in mind for desserts (the Romans liked it in cakes) or after-dinner teas. It's the key ingredient in the liqueur anisette.

ANISE HYSSOP
Agastache foeniculum

Perennial, Zones 6 to 9
This handsome perennial stands tall, usually reaching 3 to 4 feet. Its stems are square, and its leaves are bright green, oval, and pointed. In season, it is covered with 1- to 3-inch long flower spikes with purple blooms that attract large numbers of bees and butterflies.

HOW TO GROW Start anise hyssop from seeds or cuttings taken in spring or summer. It is best grown in full sun, but will tolerate some shade. Its most important requirement is well-drained soil; plants will survive in poor soil, but if the soil is enriched, anise hyssop will grow larger and have bigger blooms.

CULINARY USES Anise hyssop works well in baked goods and desserts, and as a garnish for drinks, soups, and salads; it also makes a tasty, unusual vinegar. Both the leaves and tiny blooms have a strong anise flavor. Chop leaves, use them whole, or candy them and use as a garnish. Remove each tiny flower from its calyx for a delicate taste, or strip the whole florets from the stem for a larger yield of flowers and a stronger flavor. Harvest leaves throughout the season, and flowers just before their peak bloom.

ARUGULA
Eruca vesicaria subspecies sativa

Annual
This green—also known as roquette and ruchetta—has been popular in American cuisine for quite a while, but many still find it too hot for their palate. It is a bit bitter and peppery, perhaps not surprising given the resemblance that the leaves bear to those of

Eruca vesicaria subspecies *sativa*, **arugula.**

radish. It is also related to mustards and nasturtium. The flowers, which are white with magenta veins, have the cross-shape that distinguishes mustard and other members of the crucifer family.

HOW TO GROW Plant seeds outdoors in full sun to part shade, ¼ inch deep in well-worked and moisture-retentive soil, as soon as the soil can be worked in spring. Thin them gradually (collecting them for salads or munching as you go) until they are about 6 inches apart. Like most greens, arugula doesn't like hot weather, but until summer gets serious you can keep sowing a new crop every three weeks. Resow in late summer.

CULINARY USES Add the greens to soups and salads, or sauté them with vegetables. Like spinach, they tend to be gritty, so wash them well first. Just like that green, they're a good source of vitamins A and C as well as iron. The flowers are edible, too; pinch off a few to give your salads color as well as bite. You can also use them to pretty up poultry, pasta, or vegetables.

BASIL
Ocimum basilicum

Annual

This aromatic annual has been used in the Mediterranean for thousands of years. There are now many different varieties that can reach 1 to 3 feet, with flowers ranging in color from white to pink and pale lavender. While most have bright green leaves, some varieties are splashed with purple, and there are also a number of purple or opal basils. Depending on the variety, basil tastes of anise, cinnamon, lemon, or spice, but the most popular of all is the green bush basil, which is used for making *pesto* (and the best variety for that is 'Genoa Green').

HOW TO GROW Sow seed in spring or root cuttings in spring or early summer. Basil will get by with four hours of sun, but won't really thrive without hot, full sun, and the more the better. Start seeds in a disease-free, soilless mix to control soilborne diseases that cause seedlings to wilt and collapse. Basil grows best when nights are about 70° F. It prefers a soil amended with organic matter and a near-neutral pH (6 to 6.5). Harvest leaves throughout the growing season by pinching out the tips or by cutting the plant back drastically, just above the bottom two sets of leaves. Done monthly, this will increase your yield enormously. Once plants bloom, the leaves' flavor will change, so cut the flowers back until the end of the season. Basil flowers have delicious flavor and perfume and can be used in place of the leaves.

CULINARY USES Basil is a companion plant to tomatoes in the garden and the kitchen, and it is

There are many varieties of basil, with some tasting of anise, cinnamon, and spice.

the most important ingredient for preparing *pesto*. It complements all of the seasonal vegetables like corn, eggplant, peppers, and squash. Use basil to enhance cheese dishes, fish, and fowl, as well as butters, vinegars, and oils. You can liven up any type of salad with basil. The scented basils will add interest to fruits and desserts. All of the basils are delectable, but the following varieties are among the most desirable for the cook.

Anise, licorice, or Thai basil, *O. basilicum* 'Anise', has dark green, heart-shaped leaves, light pink flowers, and a pronounced licorice flavor. It is good in salads, with cheese, fish, and fowl, and in beverages and baked goods.

Cinnamon basil, *O. basilicum* 'Cinnamon', has distinctly veined, pointed green leaves and light lavender flowers. Its aroma is clean, spicy, and cinnamony; it tastes of citrus and spice. Use it in teas, cakes, cookies, scones, or wherever you want a hint of cinnamon. Lemon basil, *O. × citriodorum* (*O. basilicum* × *O. americanum*), is available in many varieties; all are light, bright green with small white blossoms. The common lemon basil is smaller than most basils. The highly recommended varieties 'Mrs. Burns' and 'Sweet Dani' are a bit larger. All have a sweet lemon scent and taste of lemon oil with floral tones. They are delicious in iced tea and lemonade, ice cream and sorbet, baked goods, vinaigrettes, and salads, and with fish and fowl.

Opal or purple basils vary in leaf shape and texture, and size. All forms are beautiful in the garden. Their aroma and taste tend to be masked or murky due to the lack of chlorophyll, but they make a lovely garnish and are tasty when combined with green basil in salads (and they make a beautiful vinegar). Some good varieties: *O. basilicum* 'Dark Opal', 'Osmin', 'Purple Ruffles', 'Red Rubin', and 'Well-Sweep Miniature Purple'.

Sweet green basil has good-sized plants with large, bright green leaves and white flowers. This is the basil for *pesto*, to accompany tomatoes, and to use lavishly with summer vegetables and salads. *O. basilicum* 'Genoa Green Improved' tops the list, but 'Genoa Profumatissima', 'Napoletano', 'Sweet Basil' or 'Sweet Italian', and 'Valentino' also have good, well-balanced flavors.

Thai basil usually has dark green, medium-sized pointed leaves and purple flowers. Its aroma and taste is packed full of anise, spice, and citrus. *O. basilicum* 'Siam Queen' (an All-America Selection) tastes great; 'True Thai' and 'Thai Purple' are other good choices. The assertiveness of these basils enables them to hold up well in marinades, stir-fries, salads, sauces, and grilled foods.

BAY
Laurus nobilis

Perennial, Zones 8 to 11

When fresh, the scent of this noble herb combines balsam, honey, vanilla, orange, clove, and mint. Depending on growing conditions, it can be a beautiful evergreen shrub or tree.

HOW TO GROW Bay is generally grown from root cuttings because seed germination is very chancy and other methods of propagation are quite slow. Buy plants from a trustworthy grower, since bay should be well rooted, and this can take several months; or try your hand at rooting a cutting yourself. Bay prefers warm,

Laurus nobilis, bay.

humid summers, sunlight from above all year long, well-drained soil, and winter temperatures of 40° to 55° F. If you plan to grow or overwinter it indoors, a greenhouse is ideal, but a cool cellar or hallway with artificial lighting or a skylight will do fine. Bay needs full sun and consistent moisture whether indoors or out.

CULINARY USES The taste of bay is slightly sharp and peppery and somewhat bitter. Most cooks add whole leaves to long-simmering dishes at the start of cooking and remove them before serving. Fresh leaves add a subtle warmth to sweet and savory dishes. Bay is good added to stuffings of many roasted fowl dishes and adds depth and flavor to every variety of meat and most kinds of fish and shellfish. Its sweet balsamic aroma wafts from freshly baked breads and puddings. It is an essential ingredient in *bouquets garnis* for soups and stews.

BEE BALM
See description under Bergamot.

BERGAMOT
Monarda didyma

Perennial, Zones 4 to 9
Strong aroma and plentiful nectar draw bees and hummingbirds to bergamot. It's also known as bee balm and sometimes as Oswego tea, a name it earned from the fact that its fragrance is similar to that of the bergamot

Monarda didyma, bergamot.

orange (*Citrus bergamia*), used in making Earl Grey tea.

HOW TO GROW Bergamot grows from 2 to 4 feet tall in sun or partial shade, and needs mulch to keep its soil moist. Sow seed in the spring or start plants from root divisions or cuttings. Some monardas are susceptible to mildew in hot, humid summer conditions; be sure to allow plenty of air circulation and water them at ground level without wetting the foliage. Varieties resistant to mildew include 'Marshall's Delight' and 'Gardenview Scarlet'.

CULINARY USES Monarda blooms with the most perfume have the strongest flavor. The flavors of 'Cambridge Scarlet' and 'Gardenview Scarlet' are strong and flowery. Harvest both leaves and flowers throughout the season to use in cooking; the leaves have a stronger and sometimes slightly bitter flavor. Rinse the flowers gently, pat them dry, and pull individual florets from the inflorescence. These and the leaves are great with fruits, especially apricots, peaches, and plums; they work equally well in jams and jellies, baked goods, custards, and desserts. Garnish beverages and salads with the flowers.

CULTIVARS AND RELATED SPECIES The shaggy-looking, scarlet-red blooms of *M.* 'Cambridge Scarlet' and *M.* 'Gardenview Scarlet' are the most common and best known monardas. There

Borago officinalis, borage.

are also many cultivars with blooms ranging from white and coral to pink and lavender. However, these varieties as well as wild bergamot (*M. fistulosa*) do not have the same fragrance or taste as the red forms; the latter contain *carvacrol*, which is in oregano and savory, and gives them a much more pungent taste. Use small amounts of these peppery flowers and leaves in pasta salads and tomato sauce, on pizza, and with beans.

BORAGE
Borago officinalis

Annual

Anyone with a passion for blue flowers would want to grow borage for its floral display alone. The color of the sky on a perfect June day and shaped like stars, they are accentuated with black anthers and a five-part calyx with white fuzz. Stems and leaves are also fuzzy.

HOW TO GROW Sow the seeds of borage right where you want it to grow, as the plant develops a long taproot that makes it nearly impossible to transplant. It prefers full sun and fertile, well-drained soil. Make sure the bed is weeded well; borage won't tolerate competition. The mounded habit of the plant is so relaxed it could almost be described as 2 or 3 feet long rather than tall. If you're planting it as an ornamental, you won't want to situate it in a formal flower bed, but it will be right at home in your vegetable patch.

CULINARY USES The flavor of borage is inevitably compared to that of cucumbers, and the flower is the part most often consumed, added to a salad, frozen in ice cubes for a cool glass of lemonade, or candied for a snack tray or cake decoration. The tiny white hairs that add to its eye-appeal can be a turn-off to the tongue, but you can peel the stems and eat them raw or steamed. Use the leaves to flavor fish, poultry, or vegetables, then remove them before serving. Borage leaves can't be dried or frozen, but you can preserve them in vinegar to use in dressings.

BURNET
Sanguisorba minor

Perennial, Zones 3 to 8

Burnet, often called salad burnet, forms a low mound of rounded, toothed leaflets growing opposite each other on trailing stems. The overall effect is lacy enough for your flower bed. In summer, tight, rounded spikes of rosy flowers rise 2 feet above the foliage. If you find them ornamental, keep deadheading to prolong the blooming period. If the kitchen is your goal, pinch the flowers off before they bloom to net more of the leaves, which, like those of borage, taste some-

Sanguisorba minor, burnet.

what like cucumbers.

HOW TO GROW If you don't deadhead your burnet, it may self-sow. Seeds are certainly an easy way to start this plant, but if you already have some, you can divide the clump in spring. You'll want to space plants a foot or so apart. Harvest the leaves when they're young, since mature foliage will be tough and bitter. Burnet will flourish in full sun and fertile, well-drained soil.

CULINARY USES The Germans—and Thomas Jefferson—raised burnet for fodder. If you don't have cows or sheep, use burnet leaves as you would those of borage—in cool drinks (it was once added to claret to "quicken the spirits"),

Carum carvi, **caraway.**

other members of the carrot family). They are followed by the ridged seeds (more accurately, fruits), pointed at each end.

HOW TO GROW Sow caraway seeds in spring, about ½-inch deep in light, fertile soil, and thin to 8 inches apart. Keep the soil moist. Plants don't like unrelenting heat, so if you live in the South, be kind and provide a bit of shade. Mulch the biennial in fall if you live in the North. You'll want to do your best to collect all the seeds, which taste somewhere between anise and dill, so tie a bit of cheesecloth or a small paper bag around the flower head as it begins to fade. Despite your efforts, you're likely to find some volunteer seedlings the next season.

CULINARY USES Caraway seeds are most famous for their association with cabbage, notably in *sauerkraut* and slaw, and for flavoring rye bread. Try them in other baked goods like cakes and muffins, and with cheese, vegetables of all stripes, soups, and pork dishes. The seeds have been a partner for apples since the days of Shakespeare. But don't limit yourself to the seeds. The fresh leaves (which taste a bit like dill) are good in salads, and the parsnip-like root, with a spicier flavor that's more like the seeds, can be eaten raw or cooked. Caraway tea, made from steeped seeds, is said to ease upset stomachs and reduce flatulence.

salads, and vinegar—without borage's attendant fuzz. Use the leaves fresh. The pretty flowers are edible, too, and the seeds can be added to sauces and spreads.

CARAWAY
Carum carvi

Annual or biennial

Cultivated for some 5,000 years, caraway has fernlike leaves in a rosette about 15 inches tall. The biennial variety, which is more common, may remain green where winter is mild; elsewhere it will resprout from the deep taproot. The second year, white flowers borne in umbels bloom on 2-foot stalks (resembling Queen Anne's lace and

CHERVIL
Anthriscus cerefolium

Annual

Chervil's delicate flavor, a combination of parsley and anise, makes it a favorite in England and France, where it reigns with parsley and tarragon. The plant looks a bit like a miniature flat-leaved parsley with small light-green leaves, and reaches a height of about 18 inches.

HOW TO GROW Choose a partially shaded spot with very finely worked, rich soil. As soon as the soil is warm, sow the slender black seeds freely and cover lightly with fine soil, as seeds need moisture and some light for germination, which takes 10 to 14 days. Once established, chervil will do quite well and self-sow. Keep cut back to encourage new growth, or sow seeds every few weeks and again in late summer. In climates with fairly mild winters, you can keep chervil in a cold frame during the cooler months. In coastal California and in the South, sow seeds in fall for winter gardens. In strong summer heat, chervil will bolt, and its leaves will turn orange or red. 'Brussels Winter' is a slow-flowering variety, best for hot summers. Where summers are cool, chervil does well in full sun.

CULINARY USES Use chervil with fish, oysters, poultry, eggs, in salads and sauces, and with carrots, cucumbers, asparagus, avo-

Anthriscus cerefolium, chervil.

cados, mushrooms, potatoes, and melons. Many of chervil's essential oils evaporate—along with the flavor—in drying, so use it fresh or cook it only briefly. If you succeed in growing a large patch, freeze the surplus in small batches; freeze either the whole, tiny sprigs or chop it coarsely with a bit of parsley.

CHICORY
Cichorium intybus

Perennial, Zones 3 to 7

Even people who aren't interested in gardening are familiar with chicory, a roadside weed (noxious in Colorado) that looks like a tall dandelion with bright blue flowers. The leaves, which get smaller and sparser toward the top of the 3- to 4-foot plant, are toothed like a dandelion's, and chicory also has a similarly deep taproot—up to 2 feet long and 2 inches in diameter. The azure petals are square and ragged at the tip.

HOW TO GROW Give chicory a bed that has been double-dug and loaded with organic matter, in a place where it won't be disturbed by the planting and harvesting of annuals. In the North it does well in full sun, but it prefers part shade in the South. Sow the seeds ¼-inch deep in spring, thinning seedlings to about 12 inches apart. You probably won't see flowers until the second year. The leaves, which develop a distinc-

tive bite, will be less bitter if you blanch them by draping the plants with floating row covers.

CULINARY USES The Romans valued chicory as a vegetable, and the English thought it a cure for eye problems. Colonists brought it to American shores in the 17th century, primarily as a forage crop. Chicory's most famous surviving use is as a coffee flavoring; you'll need to dig and dry the root for that purpose. The fresh greens are used like a dandelion's, fresh or steamed, and are similarly nutritious.

CILANTRO
See description under Coriander.

COMMON CHIVES, GARLIC CHIVES
Allium schoenoprasum,
A. tuberosum

Perennial, Zones 3 to 9

Both common and garlic chives belong to the onion family. Common chives have cylindrical, hollow leaves, reach about 1½ to 2 feet in height, and put forth spherical, reddish purple blooms in early spring. Garlic chives (sometimes called Chinese chives) have a much stronger, garlic-like flavor. They have solid, flat leaves, can grow to 2½ feet, and much later in the season will be covered with pure white, star-shaped blooms borne on umbels.

HOW TO GROW You can propagate both types of chives by sow-

Allium schoenoprasum, **common chives.**

ing seeds in spring or by root division in spring or fall. Plant them in full sun in a well-drained soil amended with humus, in a spot with good air circulation. Garlic chives have a tendency to reseed and will grow so thickly that they choke each other out, so be sure to divide them when plantings become dense. Cut both plants back after they bloom to encourage new growth.

CULINARY USES Harvest the grass-like leaves from early spring through late fall. Use them fresh or snip them and freeze. Harvest flowers, which have a strong onion-like flavor and aroma at their peak, and use to garnish vegetables, canapés, and salads. Fresh snipped chives and their flowers flavor butters, vinegars, sauces, soups, and vegetables, and are very good with cheese and egg dishes, potatoes, tomatoes, and most vegetables. Use them to garnish foods from salads to grilled meats. Dip the whole blossoms in tempura batter and fry as an appetizer.

Coriandrum sativum, cilantro.

CORIANDER, CILANTRO
Coriandrum sativum

Annual

This herb is easy to grow and sets seed fast. The name coriander is usually applied to the seeds of the plant and cilantro to the leaves. But in some parts of the world coriander leaf or Chinese parsley refers to the foliage.

Plants have bright green foliage and can grow from 1 to 3 feet tall; when mature they send up seed stalks covered with small white flowers, which are followed by round, green seeds. Coriander is essential to Southwestern, Mexican, Thai, and Chinese cookery.

HOW TO GROW Starting in spring and continuing throughout the summer, sow coriander seed to ensure continual harvest. Plant in well-drained soil. Part shade is fine if you're growing it mainly for the leaves. The more recently introduced longer-lived varieties, such as 'Long-Standing', can grow to more than 4 feet and take longer—about 21 days—to bloom and set seed.

CULINARY USES Gather small-lobed leaves when they are young to use fresh; the later lacy foliage is also tasty, and blooms have a pungent, grassy taste. Gather seeds just before they turn brown. Add both the leaves and flowers to stir-fries, *raitas*, salads, vegetables, *salsas*, and Southwestern-style dishes like *guacamole* or *tostadas*, or use with eggs, chicken, and seafood. The flavor of coriander also goes well with dishes that include coconut milk, citrus fruits, and pineapple.

CULANTRO
Eryngium foetidum

Perennial, Zones (7) 8 to 11
This coriander smell-alike is also known as *ngo gai* (in Vietnam), *pak chee* (in Thailand), Mexican coriander, and other names that translate to stinkweed and saw-leaf herb. The last refers to its thistle-like appearance, similar to the ornamental sea holly. Culantro forms a rosette of 4-inch, sharply toothed leaves (the part that is harvested), then puts up 16-inch stalks with smaller prickly leaves and cone-shaped greenish flowers. Culantro does better in hot, humid climates than the better-known cilantro.
   HOW TO GROW Start culantro from seed indoors, since it's slow to germinate. Transplant outside in full sun to part shade, in fertile, moist, well-drained soil. Unlike real coriander, culantro is slow to

bolt (go to seed). Remove the flower stalks throughout the summer to keep production going until frost—the leaves on the stalks do become prickly and unpleasant to handle. Give it a monthly feeding of fish emulsion, protect it from hot afternoon sun, and keep a sharp eye out for slugs.
   CULINARY USES Culantro retains its flavor when dry, unlike cilantro (coriander leaf), and can be used in all the same ways—in soups, sauces, curries, and meat dishes, with rice, or in salads. Try it chopped raw and sprinkled over any south-of-the-border entree, including *tacos*, or in the Middle Eastern chickpea paste called *hummus*. Culantro is often an ingredient in a Spanish sauce called *sofrito*, which usually calls for onion, green peppers, and garlic plus other flavorings and spices, and serves as a base for sauces, soups, and meat and seafood dishes.

DILL
Anethum graveolens

Annual
Dill attracts the caterpillar of the swallowtail butterfly, which feasts on its tender foliage. Be sure to plant enough of it so that you have plenty to share with these creatures and the other beneficial insects that dill attracts. Dill's feathery, blue-green foliage grows from a thick, hollow round stem; plants reach 18 to 36 inches.

Eryngium foetidum, culantro.

Anethum graveolens, dill.

The bright yellow flowers are borne on umbels, which become heavy with flavorful seed later in the season.

HOW TO GROW Dill will grow in most climates; its requirements are sun, well-drained soil, and light fertilization. It germinates and grows quickly and may be planted after danger of frost, or year-round in suitable climates. To ensure constant leaf harvest, keep it cut back from the get-go and sow seed once a month from spring through summer. In hot, dry weather, or when dill is crowded, it will bolt. Dill's tap-roots dig down 18 inches and its branches need elbow room, so don't bother trying to grow it indoors. But it will flourish in the garden and reseed itself for years. Harvest dill throughout the season; the tender young sprigs are the best. To harvest seeds, allow the umbels to form on some plants and wait for the seeds to turn pale brown.

CULINARY USES Dill's flavor, derived from its particular camphor compound, is a mixture of anise, parsley, and celery. Use the feathery fresh leaves freely in green salads and the seeds for heavier foods—breads and potatoes. Grind seed with coarse salt to make an herb salt; store in a tightly closed container, and sprinkle on all sorts of vegetables and fish. Dill seeds taste of caraway and anise, and are great with pickles. Use dill (seeds, leaves, or both) in baked goods including breads, crackers, cookies, cakes, and pies; with fish, cheese, egg, and potato dishes; and in sauces for poultry, meats, and vegetables.

EPAZOTE
Chenopodium ambrosioides

Annual

This strongly flavored herb is also called Mexican tea, wormseed, and goosefoot. The 2-inch long, green leaves have a resinous, oily aroma, and taste somewhat like pungent winter savory. Epazote is used in Mexican and Southwestern cuisine, but is little known elsewhere.

HOW TO GROW Plant seed in

Chenopodium ambrosioides, epazote.

spring in full sun, in an enriched, well-drained soil. As the plant grows, pinch off the tips to encourage bushy growth, as it tends to be rangy and tall, reaching a height of about 4 feet. Plants will often reseed, especially in warmer regions. Harvest leaves before flowers appear; afterward, the flavor will become bitter and more like turpentine. If you allow it to go to seed you will have many volunteers in and around the garden for years to come.

CULINARY USES Epazote is used in bean and corn dishes, especially with pinto and black beans, because of its special flavor and the belief that it reduces the flatulence that can accompany bean-eating. Young epazote leaves are sometimes sautéed with wild and garden greens. Epazote's essential oils are concentrated when its leaves are dried, so use about a third the amount of dried herb as fresh. Epazote is sometimes mistaken for its relative, lambs' quarters (*Chenopodium album*)—*quelites* in Spanish, a wild green often eaten by residents of the high deserts of the Southwest.

FENNEL
Foeniculum vulgare

Perennial, Zones 4 to 10

Fennel leaves and flowers taste of mild licorice with a sweet perfume. It attracts the swallowtail butterfly caterpillar and many beneficial insects, so plant enough to share. It grows wild in warmer, sunny regions such as along the coasts of the Mediterranean, Australia, and California. Fennel is a biennial, but it sometimes behaves like a perennial when conditions are ideal, and it often self-sows. In some areas, particularly California and Virginia, fennel is invasive, so take care to contain it in your garden.

HOW TO GROW Start fennel from seed in spring or fall in full sun and rich, well-drained soil. (Do not plant fennel near dill— they can cross and will produce a plant with little flavor.) Fennel has tall, hollow stems that can easily grow to 4 to 6 feet, and its flowers are large yellow umbels. Harvest the feathery foliage of green or bronze fennel as soon as it is a few inches tall, and continue to do so throughout the season. To harvest the blooms, cut the entire umbel from the stalk, rinse the flowers, and keep the stem in water until ready to use. Harvest the brownish gray seeds for cooking or planting just before they ripen. In northern climes, dig up the taproots in autumn with a few inches of stem, overwinter them in a pot in a cold frame or root cellar, and plant out again in spring.

CULINARY USES Scatter sprigs or the flowers over salads, vegetables, or seafood. They taste best with artichokes, potatoes, tomatoes, beets, and fish, and give a

Foeniculum vulgare, fennel.

pleasing mild flavor to sauces.

CULTIVARS AND RELATED SPECIES Hardy bronze-leaved fennel (*F. vulgare* 'Bronze') adds an attractive bronze foliage to the herb garden; it also bears yellow flowers, and both are delicious to eat. Florence, or sweet fennel (*F. vulgare* var. *azoricum*) is the variety grown for the bulbs, which are eaten as a vegetable. Grow it as an annual in light, well-worked soil.

FENUGREEK
Trigonella foenum-graecum

Annual

This herb was once added to hay to cover the smell of spoilage and provide a sweet taste for its bovine and equine consumers.

Trigonella foenum-graecum, fenugreek.

Because the seeds form mucilage when wet, fenugreek has been used internally (for constipation and diarrhea) and externally (for wounds and sores).

HOW TO GROW Fenugreek is a 2-foot-tall member of the bean family with three-part leaves that make it look like clover. The off-white pea flowers have a maple-like fragrance and bloom from midsummer to fall, followed by upright pods that contain 10 to 20 seeds, the part used in cooking. After the soil has warmed in spring, sow fenugreek seeds generously where you want them to grow, thinning the seedlings to about 4 inches apart. Fenugreek prefers full sun and well-drained, organically rich soil. The seeds

should be ready to harvest in about four months.

CULINARY USES This herb is a must for Indian, Middle Eastern, and African cuisines, especially in curries and other stews, in meat and poultry, and in chutney. Use a light hand, though. While a little fenugreek is sweet and mapley (the seeds are used to make imitation maple syrup), too much makes a dish bitter. You can also use the seeds in pickling, sauté them with potatoes and other root vegetables, or sprout them to add to salads.

FRENCH TARRAGON
Artemisia dracunculus

Perennial, Zones 4 to 7

French tarragon is highly esteemed by cooks in many traditions, especially in and around Europe. The narrow pointed leaves are ¾ to 1 inch long and a bright dark green. Under the right conditions, mature plants will become handsome and bushy and 2 to 2½ feet tall. This herb is very fussy, requiring good air circulation, and will stay small and get very leggy if it isn't given the proper treatment.

HOW TO GROW Buy rooted cuttings from an herb supplier or start root cuttings yourself, because French tarragon does not come true from seed. Commercial seed is usually Russian tarragon, which lacks the essential oils valued in the kitchen. Tarragon likes a well-drained, rich soil a bit on the sandy side, and a sunny spot free from the shadow of other plants. Fertilize twice a month, especially the first few months after transplanting. Frequent cutting, especially in summer, and a mulch of sand will lessen disease problems; remove yellow or brown leaves to stop the spread of fungus. Tarragon dies back each winter even in temperate climates; in cold climates protect it with mulch. Divide plants 2 to 3 years after they are well established.

CULINARY USES The rich, anise-like, peppery flavor of tarragon enhances a variety of foods—sauces from béarnaise to tartar, eggs, fish, chicken, and grilled meats. A small amount goes well with many simply prepared vegetables, especially potatoes, peas, spinach, and cauliflower. Tarragon tastes best if used alone or as part of the classic *fines herbes*: parsley, chervil, tarragon, and chives. Heat brings out the flavor of tarragon, so use less in cooked dishes than in salads. Use tarragon fresh from the garden; it loses its flavor when dried. Tarragon is best preserved in vinegar; the flavor is true and long-lasting, though texture and color change. (See "Preserved Tarragon," page 52, for instructions.)

French tarragon.

GARLIC
Allium sativum

Perennial, Zones 4 to 9

The wonderful pungency of garlic is used in every cuisine around the world. Garlic's foliage is similar to an onion's, and plants reach 14 to 18 inches in height. If flower stalks appear, remove them to encourage underground bulb growth. Each bulb consists of six to 14 cloves.

HOW TO GROW Garlic is easy to grow. In cold climates, plant cloves about six to eight weeks before the ground freezes in fall; in temperate climates, plant when the soil is relatively dry in either January or around July and August. Garlic needs full sun and

Allium sativum, garlic.

a well-drained soil to prevent rotting. Buy bulbs for planting from a good seed supplier. Plant the individual cloves about 1½ to 2 inches deep and 6 to 8 inches apart, with the pointed end up (root end down). Mulch right away to suppress weeds; both growth and yield will be better if plants are weed-free. Harvest when leaves are brown and dry: dig up bulbs, shake free of dirt, and lay on a screen in a shady place with good air circulation. Cure garlic for two weeks before storing; the outside skins should be moisture-free. Cut off the roots and tops and store bulbs in mesh onion bags or in a box in a cool place away from light and with good air circulation, or leave tops on and braid the garlic.

CULINARY USES Use garlic fresh in marinades, soups, stews, pasta, vinaigrettes, and sauces, and with vegetables and all kinds of meat, seafood, and fowl. When cooked, garlic loses some of its pungency and turns nutty and sweet. You can also harvest young green garlic before the individual cloves form, when the plant is fresh and delicate with a tender white bulb. Pull up when it looks like a long scallion and the medium green-yellow stalks are about 12 inches long. Use green garlic anywhere garlic is called for, though you may need to use more because it is mild. Slice the fibrous stalks thinly into salads or use as a garnish or in mayonnaise. Tender whole green garlic stalks with bulbs are wonderful sautéed or baked with a little olive oil.

GARLIC CHIVES
See description under Common Chives.

LAVENDER
Lavandula angustifolia

Perennial, Zones 5 to 8
This shrubby perennial with gray-green foliage and lavender flower spikes is famous for its perfume. Most cultivars grow from 1 to 2 feet tall; on some, flower spikes reach 3 feet. Flowers and bloom time vary enormously.

Lavandula angustifolia, lavender.

HOW TO GROW Purchase plants from a reputable grower or start them from root-cuttings. Lavender needs full sun with good air circulation, well-drained soil, and regular light fertilization. Many of the less hardy lavenders do well when grown in pots. If the weather in your region is humid and your soil is heavy with clay, amend the soil with organic matter and use sand to mulch your plants. This helps with drainage, and the reflective and drying qualities of the mulch help to keep down the mold, scab, and root rot to which lavenders are susceptible. Prune plants in spring to encourage new growth. Remove spent flower stems or deadhead as flowers fade, and trim the plant back gently after it has finished flowering.

CULINARY USES Only the flowers of *L. angustifolia* are safe to eat; do not eat the foliage and never ingest the oil. Harvest the flower spikes at their peak: grasp stems in one hand and strip the flowers with forefinger and thumb of the other hand. Use them fresh or dried, but remember that the essential oils are concentrated in the dried flowers; use about a third as much as you would use fresh. These highly aromatic blooms taste very perfumey—musky with a hint of lemon. Use lavender blossoms sparingly in desserts, such as ice creams, custards, and puddings, and with fruit; they go well with

Leaf celery.

all sorts of berries. They also make interesting jellies and vinegars. The famous dried herb blend *herbes de Provence* traditionally contains lavender blossoms, thyme, summer savory, basil, and fennel seed (and sometimes marjoram, rosemary, and sage, too), and is used in cheese and egg dishes and with meat and fish, as well as in sauces and on pizza.

CULTIVARS AND RELATED SPECIES *L. angustifolia* is the best lavender for culinary use. Cultivars have flower spikes from 1 to 3 inches long, ranging from the traditional lavender to white and pink. Look for 'Folgate', 'Hidcote', 'Hidcote Pink', 'Munstead', 'Nana Alba', and 'Royal Purple'. Though beautiful in the garden, the lavandins (*Lavandula × intermedia*), *L. stoechas,* and *L. dentata* are higher in camphor and eucalyptol and do not taste good.

LEAF CELERY
Apium graveolens var. *secalinum*

Biennial grown as an annual

This variety of celery is among the "heirloom" vegetables—those grown by our ancestors and now rediscovered by modern gardeners. This plant from Europe was preserved in a seed bank in Germany. Leaf celery is sometimes called par-cel, since the handsome leaves are dark green and wavy like curly-leafed parsley, pretty enough for an ornamental bed. Other names include cutting celery and soup celery. The plants grow about 18 inches tall and, unlike most celery, don't need blanching (covering to keep them pale and tender).

HOW TO GROW Start the tiny seeds indoors 8 to 10 weeks before your last frost date, just patting them down on the surface of the growing medium. When the soil is warm outdoors, transplant them about 8 inches apart in full sun and well-amended soil. Keep them well watered, and side-dress occasionally with compost or feed with fish emulsion. The roots are shallow, so don't cultivate deeply. You can start harvesting the stalks from the outside of the plant whenever it strikes your fancy; at more than 12 inches they begin to get tough and stringy. Plants will continue producing until frost if you keep removing the outer stems.

CULINARY USES Leaf celery has a warm, rich flavor and is traditionally used in soups and stews, but it is also eaten raw or boiled. It's especially good in tomato soups and sauces. It has a stronger flavor than celery, but can be used in the same dishes, such as celery soup or Waldorf salad. Like parsley, it enhances the flavor of other herbs in such combinations as *bouquet garni*.

LEMON BALM
Melissa officinalis

Melissa officinalis 'Aurea', lemon balm.

Perennial, Zones 4 to 9

Lemon balm's botanical name comes from the Greek word for bee, as the balm patch attracts large numbers of bees when the plants are in bloom. The fragrances of lemon and sweet honey mingle in lemon balm's leaves. A member of the mint family, balm looks and grows much like mint.

HOW TO GROW Lemon balm is easy to grow from seed or rooted cuttings, or by root division. It prefers light soil, but will adapt if heavier clay soils are amended with organic matter; soil should also be fairly fertile and well balanced. Balm thrives in full sun but can be grown in partially shaded areas. (The cultivars 'All Gold' and 'Aurea' have variegated and yellow foliage, and need some shade, since full sun tends to burn them.) Because balm will compete for space, it is best planted next to other vigorous perennials that can hold their own. It grows from 2 to 2½ feet tall, bushing out laterally, so give each plant 2 feet all around. Trim plants to help maintain their handsome bushy appearance. The root system will survive cold winters if well mulched.

CULINARY USES Balm contributes a subtly sweet grassy flavor and a hint of lemon to a variety of foods. Use it fresh with vegetables, light grains, baked fish, and chicken, and in desserts. Add it near the end of cook-

Cymbopogon citratus, lemon grass.

ing, as heat dissipates its volatile oils. Balm goes well with light foods like green and fruit salads, and macerated fruits. Its fragrance keeps fairly well in baked goods because its essence is captured in the cake batter or bread dough. Crushed fresh leaves steeped with iced tea or lemonade make a delicious hot-weather beverage. For winter, dry lemon balm to make a hot tea.

LEMON GRASS
Cymbopogon citratus

Perennial, Zone 9
If you like the look of ornamental grasses, you may want to grow lemon grass just for its height and texture. It has slim, bluish green leaves and can form a clump 3 feet tall and about a foot across in a single season. Gardeners in subtropical climes where it is hardy will find that it can spread to three times that size; they will also get to enjoy the late-summer flowers—tiny and greenish white, borne in panicles that shoot up another 2 feet.

HOW TO GROW Buy a plant and grow it in a large container by itself or with other annual herbs, or use it as a "trellis" for delicate vines, such as nasturtium. It likes full sun and moisture-retentive soil that's high in organic matter. Keep it well watered, with an occasional dose of fish emulsion or liquid seaweed. The edible part is the pale swelling at the base of each leaf. Harvest the hollow stalks while they're young since they quickly become woody. If you want to grow lemon grass again the following year, divide off a clump to overwinter indoors. Just be sure to cut the blades of the new clump down to 3 or 4 inches so that the plant's energy goes to the roots and isn't spent on keeping its tall leaves alive. Handle with care—the foliage has a sharp edge.

CULINARY USES Lemon grass, an important ingredient in Vietnamese and Thai cooking, is lemony without the tangy bite of citrus. Snip the stems into sauces or soups, or use them to flavor poultry and seafood. Young leaves, like those of any lemony herb, are good in teas.

LEMON VERBENA
Aloysia triphylla

Perennial, Zones 9 to 11
This deciduous shrub is notoriously difficult to grow and not even remotely of star quality as an ornamental. The flowers are shy, retiring little lavender things with two lips; the leaves are narrow and pointed. But most of us will struggle to grow this shrub for the reason we grow many other herbs—the fragrance, a sweet, lemony perfume.

HOW TO GROW Lemon verbena rarely sets seed, so you'll need to buy a plant. Place it in full sun in a loamy, moist, but well-aerated soil. Fertilize during the growing season with fish emulsion, and keep it well pruned—weak branches can invite disease. Give it an even more severe haircut in fall. During the winter, it will drop its leaves and become dormant, so keep it just barely moist. Although the plant can easily grow to 10 feet or more where it is hardy, it will probably stop at around 5 feet for those of us who must shuffle it indoors in winter. Its lack of hardiness means that almost everyone grows it in a container. Lemon verbena is notorious for attracting whiteflies—tiny insects that swarm around greenhouses and houseplants; you may be able to control them with insecticidal soap

Aloysia triphylla, lemon verbena.

or horticultural oils.

CULINARY USES You can use chopped lemon verbena leaves whenever you need a dash of lemon—in teas, sauces, fruit salads, marinades, fish or poultry, drinks, vegetables, sauces, rice, and banana bread, to name a few. Chop them fine, since they tend to be tough, and use them with a light hand.

LOVAGE
Levisticum officinale

Perennial, Zones 4 to 8
Lovage looks like a gargantuan celery plant—up to 5 feet after three or four years—with the same U-shaped, ribbed stems and toothed, compound leaves. In

summer, tiny yellow flowers bloom in umbrella-shaped clusters up to 3 inches across, followed by ¼-inch fruits that pop open to reveal tasty, grooved seeds.

HOW TO GROW Since a little lovage goes a long way and it gets as big as a small person, a single plant is usually plenty. You can start one in spring from a division, or plant ripe seeds in fall, indoors or out. If you do plant more than one, space them at least 3 feet apart in full sun (in the South, in partial shade) in deeply worked, moist but well-drained soil. Top-dress with compost annually. You can harvest leaves and stems all season. You may notice swallowtail caterpillars feeding on the plant, but there is definitely enough greenery for sharing between humans and butterflies-to-be. Remove any leaves marred with squiggly tracks, the handiwork of leaf miners.

CULINARY USES Lovage tastes like celery, only stronger. Use it in much the same way in the kitchen as celery, but use less. Snip the leaves into salads, sauces, or soups. Use raw stems as a snack, garnish, or appetizer. Lovage teams well with potatoes and tomatoes (including in juice and spaghetti sauce). Chop it into stuffings, sauté for rice, or stir-fry or steam with other vegetables. Lovage freezes well, if you don't mind losing the crisp texture that makes it good raw.

MARJORAM
Origanum majorana

Perennial, Zones 9 to 10

Sweet marjoram has a perfume reminiscent of sweet broom (*Cytisus scoparius*), with a hint of mint and savory. It grows into a nice little bush with wiry stems, small greenish gray leaves, and small, pale purple-violet flowers in late summer or early fall.

HOW TO GROW Sweet marjoram is best propagated from root cuttings. If you start marjoram from seed, be certain that you have *O. majorana*, not *O. vulgare*—wild or winter marjoram—which is highly variable,

Levisticum officinale, lovage.

not as good a culinary herb, and sometimes rather aggressive. Sweet marjoram is perennial only in warm-temperate climates, but will grow easily in a well-drained pot that's moved indoors for the winter. In the garden, it likes good drainage and full sun, and prefers to be kept free of weeds. Fertilize about once a month. Harvest sprigs in summer and fall to use fresh or to dry.

CULINARY USES Marjoram's flavor is a well-balanced blend of sweet and slightly bitter, with a pleasant, herby aftertaste. Use the fresh leaves and flowers to flavor egg and cheese dishes, vegetables, soups, sauces, pizza, pasta, and salads. Try it in place of oregano for a milder, less pungent taste.

MINT
Mentha species

Perennial, Zones 4 to 9

Mints come in a profusion of varieties—and all tend to cross-breed with each other—which has led to much confusion among both marketers and buyers; even herb experts do not always describe the same species in the same way. To make sure that you are buying plants that are closest to the true species, buy them from trusted herb growers who take their own cuttings.

HOW TO GROW Mints cultivated from seed are notoriously vari-able. Some, such as peppermint—a sterile hybrid of *M. aquatica* and *M. spicata*—can't be grown from seed at all. Consequently, the best-quality mints come from cuttings. Plant different varieties a couple of yards apart, if possible, so they don't cross-pollinate. In small gardens, confine mints to tubs or pots buried in planting beds, or grow them as container plants, as they propagate through runners and spread throughout the garden. Water, good drainage, and a well-fertilized soil are their only growing requirements. They prefer sun but will grow in partial shade, and thrive there in very hot climates. Cut back larger plantings for drying at least three

Origanum majorana, marjoram.

Mentha suaveolens, pineapple mint.

times each season, and harvest in fall just before flowering or when the lower leaves yellow; cut the plants to the ground at this time. Hang large bunches in a shady, dry, warm spot. For small amounts, strip leaves from the stems and dry on screens.

CULINARY USES Of all of the mints, peppermints have the strongest flavor and offer great versatility for those who love mint. This variety does have a hint of pepper and is high in menthol. It is good in cooked dishes, especially in jellies and mint sauces, and makes a stimulating tea and the best mint ice cream. Spearmints are milder and sweeter than peppermints and are good in salads or wherever a lighter flavor is desired. These are the most famous mints—they are used throughout the world in every cuisine—and they are the ones associated with mint juleps, fresh mint teas, sauces, and jellies. The aroma, sweet citrus flavor, and small leaves of apple mint make it good in confections, for candying, and for punches. Orange mint is highly perfumed, with a strong citrus flavor similar to that of Earl Grey tea. It is good in iced drinks and other beverages, and as a tea, and is exceptional in fruit preserves and butters, desserts, and fruit salads.

CULTIVARS AND RELATED SPECIES Peppermint (*M. × piperita*) grows erect to about 3 feet, with bright green, pointed leaves; stems and leaves may have a deep purple-blue cast. This mint is often sold as 'Mitcham', 'Blue Balsam', 'Chocolate', and 'Black-stemmed Peppermint'. Spearmint (*M. spicata*) has many forms. Some have rounded, fuzzy, light green leaves; others have pointed, serrated bright green leaves. The plants range from 1½ to 4 feet tall. There are two varieties of apple or pineapple mint (*M. suaveolens*): one has green leaves with slight, irregular variegation in the spring; the other has green leaves with beautiful variegation all year long. Plants grow to about 2½ feet tall. Orange mint (*M. aquatica*), a lovely plant, grows to 2 to 3 feet. Its oval leaves are tinged with purple underneath; the flowers are lavender-pink. This is also called bergamot mint but should not be confused with bee balm, *Monarda didyma*.

MUSTARD
Brassica species

Annual

Many members of the genus *Brassica* are vegetables, such as cabbage and broccoli, and even mustard is more often grown as a green rather than for its tangy seeds. The condiment of the same name has been around since the days when the Romans first made it by soaking mustard seeds in wine. If you collect seeds of one of these three species, they can widen your horizons well beyond the ballpark spread.

Black mustard (*B. nigra,* a noxious weed in Massachusetts and Michigan) is the big bruiser of this bunch at 6 feet tall. White mustard (*Sinapsis alba* ssp. *alba,* formerly known as *B. hirta*) is 2 feet tall, and Chinese mustard (*B. juncea*) is a relative midget at 4 to 6 inches. All have yellow four-petaled flowers that form a cross. The leaves tend to be dark green and puckered; the lower ones are lobed.

HOW TO GROW Plant mustard seeds outdoors a couple of weeks before you expect the last frost. Give them a spot with full sun and slightly acid, moist, well-drained soil. Black mustard plants need to be at least 18 inches apart, white mustard about 12, and Chinese mustard 6 inches or more. Mustards will get hotter and more bitter during a hot, dry summer, so if you live in the South you might want to provide some shade with a trellis or taller plant, or try planting them in summer for a fall crop. Give the plants a manure or compost top-dressing, as they're greedy nitrogen consumers. The seeds usually mature in about 50 days. Try to harvest them all, since mustard can become extremely aggressive. A type of flea beetle is the most common pest, mainly in warm climates. Floating row covers (e.g., Reemay) are effective in keeping insects off. Or try dust-

Brassica nigra, black mustard.

Tropaeolum majus, nasturtium.

ing with rock phosphate or spraying with chile garlic soap.

CULINARY USES Of the three species mentioned here (and there are many more), black mustard is the spiciest (often used in Dijon spreads but not grown for greens), white mustard the mildest (used in American products), and brown mustard somewhere in between. Mustard is easily made by grinding the seeds into water, then adding vinegar or cider and other spices (hot pepper flakes if you want even more zip, turmeric to make it yellow), and finally olive oil to make it spreadable. You can also sauté the seeds with vegetables or rice; crush them into salad dressings, sauces, or marinades; use them crushed as dry "rubs" for grilling meat or whole for pickling or sprouting. Brown mustard is the most popular for greens. American southerners steam the greens of brown mustard with pork or bacon and onions. The milder white mustard greens can be used raw in sandwiches or salads.

NASTURTIUM
Tropaeolum majus

Annual

Nasturtium is so famous for spicing up the garden with its jewel tones of orange, yellow, and red that we often overlook another possibility—using the leaves (and flowers) to give peppery zip to salads and sauces. Europeans have been doing this for about 500 years, ever since the Spanish imported the plant from South America.

HOW TO GROW The species is a vine that grows to 10 feet, but more commonly grown are cultivars that form mounds or trail over the edges of containers. The wavy-edged leaves are attached by a stem in the middle, like an umbrella, and lend interest to the garden even before the flowers start blooming in midsummer. Nasturtiums start easily from seed in average or even poor soil and full sun. Plant them about 6 inches apart. Keep them well watered but be sparing with fertilizer if you want lots of flowers, and harvest leaves steadily to keep plants bushy.

CULINARY USES Put the leaves, which are loaded with vitamin C, in sandwiches as well as in salads. Add the edible flowers to salads and herbal vinegars for a splash of color. Try the unopened buds, soaked in wine or vinegar, as a substitute for capers.

NGO GAI
See description under Culantro.

OREGANO
Origanum × majoricum

Perennial, Zones 6 to 9

Cooks and herbalists alike sometimes confuse marjoram and oregano because their appearance and growing habits are so

Origanum × majoricum, oregano.

similar. It's worth sorting out the subspecies and cultivars of *Origanum,* as flavor, aroma, and cold-hardiness vary greatly. *Origanum × majoricum* is a hybrid of *O. majorana* (sweet marjoram) and *O. vulgare* and is sold as Italian oregano, oregano, or hardy marjoram. It is a hardy perennial that will survive northern winters if well mulched. There are many subspecies of *O. vulgare* that vary in size, color, flavor, and hardiness. *O. onites,* called Greek oregano and pot marjoram, has a distinctive sharp aroma that is preferred for most Greek dishes. Like marjoram, it is not winter-hardy.

HOW TO GROW True-to-type culinary oreganos are mostly

cutting-grown. Most origanums like good drainage and prefer to be kept free of weeds, with enough room around each plant for its fine-branching lateral roots. Most plants grow to between 12 and 24 inches tall and have small oval, pointed, subtly grey-green leaves, and small flowers ranging from purple to white. They do best if fertilized monthly. They will become attractively bushy if you trim them severely. Pinch or cut them back before they flower.

CULINARY USES Italian oregano, commonly cultivated in the United States, Italy, and Spain, has a more pronounced bitterness than Greek oregano, which is used in Greece, Italy, and France. The leaves of both are green with a yellowish tinge. Use either one in the kitchen when you need a burst of spice or pungency. Oregano is good in robust dishes like *chili*, soups, stews, and long-simmering ragouts, and with meat and fowl, and combines well with tomatoes in sauces, with pasta, pizza, and cheese dishes.

OSWEGO TEA
See description under Bergamot.

PARSLEY
Petroselinum species

Biennial, Zones 6 to 9
Curly parsley, *P. crispum* var. *crispum*, is the one fresh herb that is always available in North American markets. Parsley is rich in many vitamins and minerals, especially iron and vitamins A and C. Italian parsley, *P. crispum* var. *neapolitanum,* has much broader, flat leaves and a stronger flavor than the curly variety has.

HOW TO GROW Parsley seed can take from two to four weeks to germinate; soak the seeds in warm water for about a day before sowing to help speed germination. Although parsley is a biennial and will reseed itself, sow it every year for a plentiful, flavorful crop. It grows well in full sun, but some shade helps to develop a deeper green color. Plant it in rich, well-drained soil; it is a heavy feeder, requiring plenty of water and fertilizer. To harvest, cut it to about an inch above ground level, taking the outer stems first. Always use parsley fresh since it is so easy to grow or buy and much of its flavor is lost when it is dried or frozen. Parsley is very hardy and may be used well into winter, even when the leaves have frozen.

CULINARY USES A bite of fresh parsley reveals a bright flavor with a faint peppery tang and a green-apple aftertaste. The brilliance of its emerald green leaves and its mild yet piquant flavor have made it a standard garnish. This herb is difficult to overuse. It is pleasant with most vegetables, fish, and meats; in butters, sauces, and dressings; and in dishes from fresh salads to long-simmered ragouts.

PEPPERMINT
See description under Mint.

PERILLA
Perilla frutescens

Annual

Cooks usually refer to this plant as shiso (or tia to). Gardeners commonly call it beefsteak mint, and environmentalists in the mid-Atlantic call it a noxious weed, since it's highly invasive there. Unlike other members of the mint family that wear out their welcome spreading by underground runners, this annual just seeds itself around too eagerly.

HOW TO GROW Closely related to basil (it's also called Japanese basil), perilla has similar quilted, green leaves but with jagged edges. The late-summer white flowers, borne on spikes like basil's, are small and relatively insignificant. Snip off the flower spikes to keep perilla from taking over your beds and to prevent the leaves from becoming bitter. Perilla germinates readily from seed in almost any soil and will grow in shade, although sun makes it more robust.

CULINARY USES Perilla is used in salads, and in Japanese cooking it is popular as a garnish for *tempura* and to make wrappings for *sushi* and *sashimi*. Salted, it is a condiment for tofu.

Italian parsley.

Perilla frutescens, perilla.

CULTIVARS AND RELATED SPECIES
There is a botanical variety of perilla (*P. frutescens* var. *crispa*) with bronze or purple foliage, and a cultivar (*P. frutescens* 'Atropurpurea') with reddish purple leaves. The foliage of these plants lends interesting color to an ornamental border (much like coleus, to which they are closely related). But the species is considered more aromatic and better for culinary uses.

PINEAPPLE SAGE
Salvia elegans

Perennial, Zones 8 to 11
If common sage smacks of Thanksgiving stuffing or you find its flowers too blue, try this more tender relative, even if it means

Salvia elegans, **pineapple sage.**

hauling it indoors in winter. Like *S. officinalis,* it's shrubby in nature, sometimes growing to 6 feet where it is hardy, and 2 to 3 feet elsewhere. The late-season flowers are deep-throated and fire-engine red (just the sort that drive hummingbirds into a frenzy), especially those of the cultivar 'Scarlet Pineapple'. The scent and taste are fruity with pineapple overtones.

HOW TO GROW Unless you live in Zone 8 or south, you probably should grow pineapple sage in a container. Like common sage, it's slow to take off from seed, so save yourself some time and buy a plant, or talk a friend out of a cutting. It grows best in full sun in rich, slightly acid soil. Salvias aren't fussy to grow, as long as they have good drainage. Give this one some organic fertilizer during the growing season, and be sure it has a lot of sun when you bring it indoors.

CULINARY USES The leaves of pineapple sage go well with seafood and poultry, with apples and pears, and in jellies or fruit drinks, muffins, or other breads. Or put its fruity taste to work with vegetables, such as squash, carrots, or green beans. The flowers are also edible—they taste more fruity and less "sagey" than the leaves. They give a real spark to fruit salads, teas and other beverages, or desserts.

RAU NGO, RAU OM
Limnophila aromatica

Perennial, Zones 10 to 11
This semi-trailing plant, which first came to the United States with Vietnamese refugees in the 1970s, is a member of a wide-ranging family that includes mostly subtropical and tropical plants but also our native penstemons and turtleheads, garden favorites like veronicas and snapdragons, and the purple-flowering paulownia tree. Rau ngo grows 12 to 15 inches tall with succulent stems and small, widely spaced leaves in whorls of three. The pale lavender-blue summer flowers, borne at the ends of the stems, are ½-inch across with cream-colored throats.

HOW TO GROW Members of this genus are all native to wetlands. Rau ngo is often called rice paddy plant because that's where it's cultivated in Vietnam. It doesn't necessarily need swampy conditions, but give it soil that never dries out, plenty of mulch, and protection from hot afternoon sun, plus an occasional feeding with fish emulsion. It can be difficult to overwinter where indoor air is dry. Mist it or set the pot in a saucer of water. You can start it from stem cuttings purchased at Asian markets.

CULINARY USES The Vietnamese use the leaves, which have a distinctive musky, citrus-floral scent reminiscent of

Limnophila aromatica, rau ngo.

patchouli, in sweet-and-sour dishes and curries. The unique tang calls for experimentation with shellfish and other strong fish, pork, and duck, roasted vegetables, or vegetable soups. It is often paired with lemon grass. Be careful not to overdo it, though, because the perfumey undertaste can be overpowering.

ROQUETTE
See description under Arugula.

ROSEMARY
Rosmarinus officinalis

Perennial, Zones 8 to 10
From the cook's point of view, all the many varieties of *R. officinalis* are useful, whether they are

thin- or thick-leaved, pink- or blue-flowered. Each variety has a unique aroma and flavor, and differing physical characteristics such as plant and leaf size, variegation, flower color, and cold-hardiness.

HOW TO GROW A cutting is the best way to start rosemary, as seed germination is slow. Rooted cuttings are available from herb growers, or you can propagate them easily yourself. Rosemary needs light but regular watering and misting. Fertilize monthly, whether outside or inside. Let plants dry between watering; if plant tips turn brown you have overwatered. During summer, prune monthly or as needed to

Rosmarinus officinalis, **rosemary.**

maintain good air circulation, which is necessary to prevent powdery mildew, especially in humid climates. Rosemary is a true Mediterranean plant and will not survive extremely cold winters, but a number of varieties are pretty cold-hardy, if protected. In warm southern or coastal regions, cut plants back in fall and spring.

You can grow rosemary in pots and keep it indoors during cold weather. Plant in roomy containers in a mix of potting soil or humus plus perlite or large-grained, sterile sand for good drainage. Set plants outdoors in the spring and leave them out all summer, watering well. About a month before the first frost, bring plants to a protected area near the house, and move them to a cool spot inside two weeks later, before you turn on the heat, giving plants time to adjust. On mild winter days, hauling rosemary plants in and out does them wonders, as they appreciate the fresh air.

CULINARY USES Rosemary's moderate bitterness and peppery flavor are especially good with foods rich in fat, such as roast meats, poultry, and fish; or with bland foods, such as potatoes or legumes. Use it in long-simmered dishes, soups, and stews. Mince fresh rosemary or add sprigs that can be removed before serving. Dry rosemary sprigs whole to preserve the oils, but crumble it when cooking or tie it into cheesecloth so that you won't feel

as if you are chewing on pine nee-
dles. The strength of the dried
herb varies greatly; generally, use
one-third as much as you would
use fresh.

**CULTIVARS AND RELATED
SPECIES** A low-growing tender
variety, *R. officinalis* var. *prostra-
tus*, makes a fine groundcover,
growing from 6 to 12 inches tall
and spreading easily, while some
of the upright varieties can reach
6 feet in height. Some varieties
that can survive the winter at
least to Zone 7 are 'Arp', 'Hill
Hardy', 'Salem', 'Nancy Howard',
and 'Dutch Mill'.

RUCHETTA
See description under Arugula.

SAFFRON
Crocus sativus

Perennial, Zones 6 to 9
Ever tried to buy saffron for
your *paella* and had the grocer
tell you to wait while she opened
the safe? The little threads in the
bottle she pulled from the safe's
confines are the stigmas of a fall-
blooming crocus, and it takes an
estimated 60,000 flowers to make
a pound of saffron. So you aren't
likely to get rich from growing
your own, but you can enjoy the
surprising 2-inch lilac-colored
flowers, which have purple veins
and throats and orange-red stigmas for added drama. Any spice
you collect will be a bonus.

Crocus sativus, saffron crocus.

Salvia officinalis 'Purpurascens', sage.

HOW TO GROW Saffron grows from modified bulbs called corms, which should be planted 3 to 4 inches deep and 6 inches apart in spring or early summer. Give them full sun to part shade, in light, gritty, average soil. You can fertilize with a pinch of rock phosphate, but make sure that the fertilizer doesn't touch the corms or it may burn them. Saffron doesn't like wet or humid climates, and can't take the heat south of Zone 8.

CULINARY USES Saffron is famous as an ingredient in the French seafood stew known as *bouillabaisse* as well as in the Spanish rice combo called *paella*. A little goes a long way, fortunately, but if you decide to harvest your own saffron crop, be sure to dry the stigmas carefully and store them in an airtight container in a cool place.

SAGE
Salvia officinalis

Perennial, Zones 5 to 8
The soft, gray-green foliage of sage provides a pleasing contrast to the bright hues of many other culinary herbs. In season, common sage (*S. officinalis*) has spikes laden with purple blooms. Different varieties have pink or white flowers, or variegated leaves. Common sage grows as a bush to about 2 to 3 feet tall and 3 feet in diameter, keeping a well-rounded shape with little pruning in mild climates.

HOW TO GROW Sage needs a well-drained or gravelly soil; add calcium if it is lacking in your soil. It also prefers full sun but will take some shade, provided it has good air circulation. Mulch plants with an inch or two of sand or chicken grit (a mixture of coarsely ground granite and oyster shells); the light-colored, reflective mulch adds heat and dries out the center of the plant, reducing the chance of disease. Once established, sage is hardy and needs little care. Mulch it well if winters in your area are very cold. Whether you are growing it in a pot or the garden, prune it in early spring to encourage new growth. Harvest leaves throughout the summer to use fresh, or dry them.

CULINARY USES Known as a digestive, sage is often found in rich dishes. Besides its traditional uses in sausages and with poultry, game, and liver, sage is good with cheeses, vegetables, breads, and sweets. Crumble dry sage as needed for cooking; do not grind it as this completely destroys its delicate lemony perfume while its harsher, resinous flavors remain.

CULTIVARS AND RELATED SPECIES Both sturdy and robust, *S. officinalis* 'Berggarten', with rounded leaves, and *S. officinalis* 'Purpurascens', with grayish purple foliage, look wonderful in the herb garden, and are similar in flavor to common sage. The variegated and golden sages are also beautiful, but are milder and don't make good culinary choices.

See Pineapple sage, page 90.

SAVORY
Satureja species

Semi-evergreen perennial (winter savory, Zones 4 to 8); annual (summer savory)

Winter and summer savories are members of the mint family, with erect stems and narrow leaves about an inch long. Summer savory (*S. hortensis*), the annual, grows to 18 inches tall and is smothered in tiny pale pink flowers. The slightly fuzzy leaves are gray-green and sometimes turn purple in autumn before giv-

Satureja montana, winter savory.

ing up the ghost. Winter savory (*S. montana*), a hardy perennial, can become somewhat shrubby in habit but grows to a foot and a half tall, with spikes of white or lavender flowers that may have darker purple spots. The leaves are darker green and taste more peppery than those of summer savory.

HOW TO GROW Either plant can be started from seed, but since the perennial, winter savory, is slow to mature, it's easier to buy a plant. Space plants of either species about a foot apart. Summer savory may be the more difficult to grow, since it droops if water-deprived and bolts (goes to seed) quickly in hot climates. Harvest it regularly in spring, since it may not be around by late summer. Do the

same for its perennial cousin, as regular pruning will keep it bushy and productive. You can start new plants of winter savory from cuttings or divisions and probably should, since the plant tends to be short-lived. Both species prefer full sun and well-drained, neutral to slightly acid soil.

CULINARY USES Savory combines the flavors of thyme and mint and is often paired with beans, peas, or lentils. Dried, it can be added to stuffing or breading for chicken, fish, or pork. Try it in marinades or with eggs, or steeped in vinegar for dressings. Keep in mind that the flavor of winter savory is somewhat stronger (some find it almost piney) and use less of it, or save it

Pelargonium 'Mabel Gray', a geranium with a lemon verbena-like scent.

for stronger flavored meats such as game, crabmeat, or bluefish.

SCENTED GERANIUM
Pelargonium species

Perennial, Zones 10 to 11
Even if you don't use any of your herbs—although of course "use" is the key word defining an herb—you will find that most of them are worth growing for the pungency of their leaves. This is especially true of the scented geraniums, which have the scent of roses, coconut, apples, lemon, cedar, and many other aromas that are harder to describe. They can be the size of small shrubs or droop demurely over the edge of a hanging basket. Leaves that are variegated, fuzzy, scalloped, or lobed add to their appeal. Flowers can be showy red, pink, lavender, and bicolored, or small white afterthoughts.

HOW TO GROW Geraniums root readily from cuttings in damp sand or even just water, so it's easy to get started if you have a friend who collects these charming plants. Grow them in containers that you can move indoors in winter, and give them some organic fertilizer in summer. Otherwise, just make sure they have good drainage and enough water to keep them from wilting, and don't hesitate to prune those that are getting too big or lanky.

CULINARY USES The most common use for the leaves is in *pot-pourri*, but you can let their scent inspire you in the kitchen, too. Rose-scented geranium leaves are often used to enliven jellies. Or add the leaves to cakes or mix them with sugar for a couple of weeks for a surprising rosy flavor. The leaves of mint- and lemon-scented geraniums can be used in teas or in any other ways that you might employ those flavors.

SORREL
Rumex acetosa, R. scutatus

Perennial, Zones 4 to 8
R. acetosa, garden sorrel, grows 2 to 4 feet tall, with long, dark green leaves and rust-colored flower spikes in early summer. *R. scutatus,* which is often referred to

Rumex scutatus, **French sorrel.**

Vietnamese coriander.

as French sorrel, has a spear-shaped, pale green leaf and is the best for cooking. It flowers in early summer and again in fall, and grows from 12 to 24 inches tall.

HOW TO GROW Sorrel grows best in full sun in a rich well-drained soil, but will do moderately well in partial shade. Harvest throughout the season by cutting it back continually. If the leaves dry out in hot weather, they can taste a little bitter; mulch plants well to retain moisture. Cut back seed stalks throughout the summer. In hot, humid conditions the plant will die back, but it will re-emerge as the weather cools. Sorrel has a deep root system that can be divided in spring or fall.

CULINARY USES It is a French tradition to indulge a taste for sorrel in spring—in fact, cream of sorrel soup and sorrel sauce are considered spring tonics. Sorrel's slightly sour flavor with a lemony zest sparks the palate like no other herb. Sorrel is good with eggs and vegetables, and in sauces or mayonnaise. Add young leaves by the handful to make simple salads lively. Cooked dishes that include sorrel need less salt, and salads need little or no vinegar or lemon juice when made with sorrel. Leaves smaller than 6 inches are best in salads; larger ones are better cooked or combined with other foods. To retain sorrel's bright green color in soups and sauces, cook it just briefly. Sorrel has particularly thin leaves and does not freeze or dry well, so enjoy it in spring or early summer when it's in season.

SPEARMINT
See description under Mint.

SUMMER SAVORY
See description under Savory.

TARRAGON
See description under French Tarragon.

VIETNAMESE CORIANDER
Polygonum odoratum

Perennial, Zones 9 to 11
Like other members of this genus, commonly called

knotweeds, this herb has joined, somewhat zig-zagging stems, often touched with red when new. The lance-shaped leaves can also be streaked with burgundy.

HOW TO GROW Start Vietnamese coriander, also known as rau ram, from cuttings—an obvious source is a Vietnamese market. In fall, take more cuttings or divisions to overwinter indoors under lights or in a sunny window. It grows about a foot tall, then spreads, and thus makes an attractive houseplant in a hanging basket. It has a reputation for being aggressive, although this shouldn't be a problem north of Zone 9.

CULINARY USES As you might guess from the common name, Vietnamese coriander tastes similar to coriander. But it has its own piquant undertones, which even some admirers compare to soap. The leaves are often paired with chicken—in salads or stir-fries—or used in brothy soups. They are also used in a dipping sauce where they are mixed with fish sauce, garlic, and lime.

WATERCRESS
Nasturtium officinale

Perennial, Zones 6 to 9

Of the several varieties of cress, watercress is the best known and most commonly available, found in markets in spring and fall. It grows in moving streams where its free-rooting stems have a tendency to spread.

Nasturtium officinale, watercress.

Watercress grows from 6 to 18 inches tall. The spicy, slightly bitter, dark green leaves are best harvested before the plant's white flowers appear in summer. Do not eat cress unless you are sure that the stream contains no human or animal contaminants.

HOW TO GROW Because watercress requires very rich, marshy earth, flowing water, and protection from the cold, it is usually cultivated commercially. Unless you are lucky enough to have a stream running through your garden, growing watercress will be difficult. If you want to have a go at growing watercress but don't have a stream, try sowing the seeds in pots or flats in a rich growing medium. You will need to place the pots or containers in water and change it daily. Cress likes full sun or part shade.

CULINARY USES The rich, holly-green color of cress indicates the many minerals and vitamins that it contains. Though it is not an aromatic herb, the peppery flavor adds interest to salads and soups. Most popular as a salad herb, it enlivens any green or vegetable salad and those made with grains, potatoes, pasta, fish, or chicken. Cooking decreases its pungency and reveals an agreeable herbal, vegetable taste, with overtones of spinach, parsley, and mustard greens.

WINTER SAVORY
See description under Savory.

Galium odoratum, woodruff.

WOODRUFF
Galium odoratum

Perennial, Zones 3 to 8

This may not be the most useful herb in the kitchen, but it makes up for that with its amenability in the garden. Who couldn't use a low-care, shade-loving groundcover with delicate whorls of leaves and fragrant white flowers? The plant may reach 9 inches high; the leaves are 1 to 2 inches across. When the foliage dries, it develops its signature scent of honey and vanilla.

HOW TO GROW Woodruff is difficult to start from seed, so buy some plants or look for a friend who will share some divisions with you. Then give them shade and rich, humusy soil that doesn't dry out. If you want woodruff to spread more quickly, divide the plants in spring, making sure that each division has a generous amount of root attached.

CULINARY USES Sweet woodruff is best known for flavoring *Maibowle*, a wine drink made with white wine and served in Germany on May 1 to welcome spring. You can use it to the same effect by soaking a few sprigs in an inexpensive white wine for a few days.

THYME
Thymus species

Perennial, Zones 4 to 8

Of the many kinds of common thyme (*T. vulgaris*) available for

Thymus × *citriodorus,* lemon thyme.

culinary use, the French and English varieties—which have very similar aromatic properties—are most popular. Choose named varieties such as 'Broad-leaf English' or 'Narrow-leaf French'. These small, woody perennials are evergreen and range from 6 to 18 inches tall.

HOW TO GROW Thymes grow best in sandy soil, as their root structures are very fine and unable to find enough nutrients in heavy soil. They prefer full sun and don't like to be wet, so work sand and gravel into the soil to ensure good drainage. Mulch with sand, light-colored gravel, or chicken grit to reflect heat up to the plant, reducing moisture and the chance that plants will develop diseases. Divide favorite plants in spring or early fall and take root cuttings in summer. Prune thymes several times a year, especially where summers are hot and humid.

CULINARY USES Thyme has hints of mint, bay, and marjoram. It goes well with grains, especially rice and pasta; meat, fowl, and eggs; and most vegetables, especially potatoes, carrots, squash, onions, and tomatoes. It is delicious with shellfish and fish. Thyme enhances the simplest soup or stew and works well with winter fruits and in salads. It is essential in *bouquets garnis* for making stock. During drying, thyme will lose some of its fragrance, and will attain an earthy aroma and pungent flavor.

CULTIVARS AND RELATED SPECIES The lemon thymes (*T. × citriodorus,* Zones 5 to 9) are a little less hardy than common thyme, but add a wonderful lemon scent and flavor to the garden and kitchen. They too, grow in compact bushes, and come in a variety of leaf colors from green to gold to variegated. Caraway thyme (*T. herba-barona*), a low-growing, scented variety, has hints of caraway and nutmeg. Use these fragrant herbs fresh, with little or no cooking. They are excellent in marinades. There are many other varieties and cultivars of *Thymus,* including the creeping thymes, which are beautiful groundcovers but are not useful in the kitchen.

Thyme and oregano soften the contours of the garden and are drought-tolerant.

USDA HARDINESS ZONE MAP

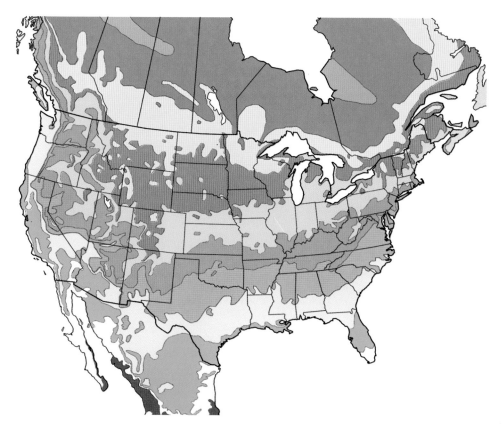

ZONES & MINIMUM WINTER TEMPERATURES (°F.)

Zone 1 below –50°

Zone 2 –50° to –40°

Zone 3 –40° to –30°

Zone 4 –30° to –20°

Zone 5 –20° to 10°

Zone 6 –10° to 0°

Zone 7 0° to 10°

Zone 8 10° to 20°

Zone 9 20° to 30°

Zone 10 30° to 40°

Zone 11 above 40°

SEED & PLANT SOURCES

COMPANION PLANTS
7247 North Coolville Ridge Road
Athens, Ohio 45701
740-592-4643, 740-593-3092 fax
complants@frognet.net
www.companionplants.com/

THE COOK'S GARDEN
P.O. Box 5010
Hodges, S.C. 29653-5010
800-457-9703, 800-457-9705 fax
orders@cooksgarden.com
www.cooksgarden.com/

JOHNNY'S SELECTED SEEDS
Foss Hill Road
Albion, Maine 04910
207-437-4301
homegarden@johnnyseeds.com
www.johnnyseeds.com/

NATIVE SEEDS/SEARCH
526 N. 4th Avenue
Tucson, AZ 85705-8450
520-622-5561
info@nativeseeds.org
nativeseeds.org

NICHOLS GARDEN NURSERY
1190 Old Salem Road NE
Albany, Oregon 97321-4580
541-928-9280, 800-231-5306 fax
www.nicholsgardennursery.com/

PARK SEED COMPANY
1 Parkton Avenue
Greenwood, SC 29649
800-213-0076
info@parkseed.com
www.parkseed.com/

THE REDWOOD CITY SEED COMPANY
P.O. Box 361
Redwood City, CA 94064
650-325-7333
www.batnet.com/rwc-seed/

RENEE'S GARDEN
7389 West Zayante Road
Felton, CA 95018
888-880-7228
www.reneesgarden.com/

RICHTERS HERBS
357 Highway 47
Goodwood
Ontario, Canada L0C 1A0
905-640-6677, 905-640-6641
orderdesk@richters.com
www.richters.com/

SANDY MUSH HERB NURSERY
316 Surrett Cove Road
Leicester, NC 28748-5517
828-683-2014
www.brwm.org/sandymushherbs/

SEED SAVER'S EXCHANGE
3076 North Winn Road
Decorah, Iowa, 52101
319-382-5990, 319-382-5872 fax

SEEDS OF CHANGE
P.O. Box 15700
Santa Fe, NM 87506-5700
888-762-7333
gardener@seedsofchange.com
store.yahoo.com/seedsofchange/

SHEPHERD'S GARDEN SEED
30 Irene St.
Torrington, CT 06790-6658
860-482-3638
www.shepherdseeds.com/

WELL-SWEEP HERB FARM
205 Mount Bethel Road
Port Murray, NJ 07865
908-852-5390
908-852-1649 fax

FOR MORE INFORMATION

BASIL: AN HERB LOVER'S GUIDE
Thomas DeBaggio & Susan Belsinger
DK Publishing, 1999

THE BIG BOOK OF HERBS
Arthur Tucker & Thomas DeBaggio
Interweave Press, 2000

THE EDIBLE HERB GARDEN
Rosalind Creasy
Periplus Editions, 1999

THE ENCYCLOPEDIA OF HERBS, SPICES, AND FLAVORINGS
Elisabeth Lambert Ortiz
DK Publishing, 1992

ENCYCLOPEDIA OF HERBS AND THEIR USES
Deni Bown
DK Publishing, 1995

EXOTIC HERBS: A COMPENDIUM OF EXCEPTIONAL CULINARY HERBS
Carole Saville
Henry Holt, 1997

EYEWITNESS HANDBOOKS: HERBS
Lesley Bremness
DK Publishing, 1994

GROWING HERBS FROM SEED, CUTTING, AND ROOT: AN ADVENTURE IN SMALL MIRACLES
Thomas DeBaggio
Interweave Press, Revised Edition, 2000

HERBS FOR DUMMIES
Karan Cutler Davis & Kathleen Fisher
IDG Books, 2000

HERBS IN THE KITCHEN: A CELEBRATION OF FLAVOR
Carolyn Dille & Susan Belsinger
Interweave Press, 1992

HERBS, SPICES, AND FLAVORINGS
Tom Stobart
Overlook Press, 2000

PARK'S SUCCESS WITH HERBS
Gertrude Foster & Rosemary Louden
Scribner, 1982

SOUTHERN HERB GROWING
Madalene Hill & Gwen Barclay
Shearer Publishing, 1997

CONTRIBUTORS

SUSAN BELSINGER is a food writer, educator, and photographer. Her work has appeared in publications including *Gourmet, Herb Companion, Kitchen Gardener, Natural Home, Organic Gardening,* and the *Washington Post.* She is the author of *Basil: An Herb Lover's Guide, The Garlic Book, Flowers in the Kitchen, Herbs in the Kitchen*, and many other books. She gives lectures and demonstrations on herbs, cooking, and gardening throughout the U.S. and Canada.

KARAN DAVIS CUTLER grows herbs, vegetables, fruits, and flowers in northern Vermont. A former magazine editor, her most recent books are *Herb Gardening for Dummies* (IDG Books, 2000, with Kathleen Fisher) and *The New England Gardener's Book of Lists* (Taylor Publishing Co., 2000). She's also the editor of four Brooklyn Botanic Garden handbooks: *Salad Gardens* (1995), *Tantalizing Tomatoes* (1997), *Starting from Seed* (1998), and *Flowering Vines* (1999).

KATHLEEN FISHER, former editor of *The American Gardener*, is the author of several gardening books including the recent *Herb Gardening for Dummies*, with Karan Davis Cutler, *Complete Guide to Water Gardens* (Creative Homeowner Press), *Herbal Remedies: Dozens of Safe, Effective Treatments to Grow and Make* (Rodale's Essential Herbal Handbooks), and *Taylor's Guide to Shrubs* (Houghton Mifflin). She lives in Alexandria, Virginia.

BETH HANSON is former managing editor of the Brooklyn Botanic Garden's 21st-Century Gardening Series. She is the editor of the BBG handbooks *Easy Compost* (1997), *Chile Peppers* (1999), and *Natural Disease Control* (2000), and contributed to *The Brooklyn Botanic Garden Gardener's Desk Reference* (Henry Holt, 1998). She lives outside of New York City and writes about gardening, health, and the environment for various publications.

MADALENE HILL and her daughter, GWEN BARCLAY, wrote *Southern Herb Growing,* (Shearer Publishing) and their work has appeared in *The Houston Post's Houston at Home* magazine, *The Herb Companion, The Herb Quarterly, Neil Sperry's Gardens, Texas Gardener,* and several other publications. Madalene Hill is past president of The Herb Society of America. Gwen Barclay chaired both the Society's South Texas and Pioneer units. Together they were instrumental in the formation of the Texas Herb Growers & Marketers Association; Gwen served as its organizational chairman and first president for three years, and is now director of food service for the Festival Institute in Round Top, Texas.

BARBARA PERRY LAWTON, garden editor of *St. Louis Homes & Life Styles*, is a writer, garden consultant, photographer, and public relations counselor. She is a former manager of publications for Missouri Botanical Garden, and for 18 years wrote a weekly garden column for the St. Louis-based *Post-Dispatch*. She is the author of *A Seasonal Guide to the Natural Year in Illinois, Missouri and Arkansas,* and *Magic of Irises* (both published by Fulcrum). Timber Press will be publishing Lawton's latest book, tentatively titled *Mints.*

HOLLY SHIMIZU is the executive director of the U.S. Botanic Garden in Washington, D.C. and the former managing director for Lewis Ginter Botanical Garden near Richmond, Virginia. She served as editorial consultant on the *Eyewitness Handbook: Herbs* (DK Publishing, 1994) and was a co-author of *The American Garden Guide Book on Herb Gardening* (Pantheon, 1994). She is one of the hosts of the television show, "Victory Garden," and developed "Holly Shimizu's Video Guide to Growing and Using Herbs."

ILLUSTRATIONS AND PHOTOS

Cover background illustrations by PAUL HARWOOD
Three Herb Garden Designs by STEVE BUCHANAN
DAVID CAVAGNARO cover, pages 1, 5, 23, 33, 43, 49, 51, 58, 61, 62, 63, 64, 65, 66, 67, 68, 69, 72, 73, 75, 76, 77, 80, 81, 82, 83, 84, 86, 87, 89 left, 94, 95, 97, 99, 102
DEREK FELL pages 7, 8, 11 all, 13 top and bottom, 16, 32, 36, 39, 47, 52, 78, 85, 89 right, 93
GWEN BARCLAY & MADALENE HILL pages 9, 34, 37, 38, 48, 53, 71 left, 74, 91, 98
JERRY PAVIA pages 19, 21, 71 right, 79, 96
JUDY WHITE/GARDENPHOTOS.COM pages 20, 59
ALAN & LINDA DETRICK pages 28, 46, 50, 100
SUSAN BELSINGER pages 40, 42, 55
ELVIN McDONALD page 54
SUSAN M. GLASCOCK pages 90, 101
CHARLES MANN page 92

INDEX

BROOKLYN BOTANIC GARDEN

MORE BOOKS

ON KITCHEN

GARDENING

JOIN THE
BROOKLYN BOTANIC GARDEN
OR **GIVE** A GIFT
OF MEMBERSHIP

Here are the membership benefits you can enjoy and share with others:

SUBSCRIBER $35

- Subscriptions to *21st-Century Gardening Series* handbooks and *Plants & Gardens News*
- Use of Gardener's Resource Center
- Reciprocal privileges at botanical gardens across the country

INDIVIDUAL $35

- One membership card for free individual admission
- 10% discount at the Garden Gift Shop
- Entry to members' summer hours, Sunset Picnics, and Preview Night at the Plant Sale
- Discounts on adult classes, trips, and tours
- *BBG Members News* and course catalog mailings
- Use of Gardener's Resource Center
- Reciprocal privileges at botanical gardens across the country

FAMILY/DUAL $65

All of the above INDIVIDUAL benefits, plus
- 2 membership cards for free admission for 2 adults & their children under 16
- Free parking for 4 visits
- 10% discount at the Terrace Cafe
- Discounts on children's programs and classes
- Subscriptions to *21st-Century Gardening Series* handbooks and *Plants & Gardens News*

FAMILY/DUAL PLUS $95

All of the above, plus
- 1 guest admitted free each time you come
- Free parking for 8 visits
- 2 SUBSCRIBER gift memberships for the price of one

SIGNATURE $150

All of the above, plus
- Your choice of one Signature Plant
- Free parking for 12 visits
- A special BBG gift calendar

SPONSOR $300

All of the above, plus
- Your choice of 2 Signature Plants
- 4 complimentary one-time guest passes
- Free parking for 18 visits

PATRON $500

All of the above, plus
- 2 guests admitted free each time you come
- Recognition in selected printed materials
- Free parking for 24 visits

GAGER SOCIETY $1500

All of the above, plus
- Unlimited free guests each time you come
- Gager Society Dinner and garden trip
- Complimentary INDIVIDUAL gift membership for a friend
- Private receptions for higher level donors
- Unlimited free parking for a year

Please use the form on reverse to join.
For more information, call the Membership Department: 718-623-7210

MEMBERSHIP FORM

Your Name

Address

City   State   Zip   Membership #

Daytime phone   Evening phone

email   ☐ Check if this is a renewal.

Please enroll me as a member of the Brooklyn Botanic Garden.

☐ Subscriber $35   ☐ Signature $150
☐ Individual $35   ☐ Sponsor $300
☐ Family/Dual $65   ☐ Patron $500
☐ Family/Dual Plus $95   ☐ Gager Society $1500

Please send a gift membership to the recipient below.

☐ Subscriber $35   ☐ Signature $150
☐ Individual $35   ☐ Sponsor $300
☐ Family/Dual $65   ☐ Patron $500
☐ Family/Dual Plus $95   ☐ Gager Society $1500

Gift Recipient's Name

Address

City   State   Zip

Daytime phone   Evening phone

email

Method of Payment

☐ Check (payable to Brooklyn Botanic Garden)
☐ Visa ☐ MasterCard ☐ AMEX

Card #   Exp. Date

Signature

Please tear along perforation, complete form and return with payment to:
Membership Office, Brooklyn Botanic Garden,
1000 Washington Avenue, Brooklyn, NY 11225-1099
Phone: 718-623-7210 Fax: 718-857-2430